The Land and People of
JORDAN

The Kingdom of Jordan is a new country with an ancient past. It includes the oldest city in the world, Jericho, and the Biblical regions of Gilead, Moab, and Edom. It has castles held by the Crusaders when they fought to free the Holy Land from the Muslims, and cities sacred to three great faiths: Judaism, Christianity, and Islam.

Today, under the leadership of its young king, Hussein I, Jordan is trying to cope with the problems brought about by the influx of thousands of Palestinian refugees, even while conflict with its neighbor, Israel, persists. The government is making every effort to modernize the country under these difficult circumstances. It is building roads to its only port, Aqaba; dams to use its most precious resource, water; and schools and hospitals.

In this thoroughly revised edition Frances Copeland Stickles gives us a vivid look at this desert country and its people, and the problems it faces in dealing with the warp of old heritages and the woof of new alliances and political complexities.

PORTRAITS OF THE NATIONS SERIES

The Land and People of

JORDAN

by Paul W. Copeland
revised by Frances Copeland Stickles

REVISED EDITION 1972

PORTRAITS OF THE NATIONS SERIES

J. B. LIPPINCOTT COMPANY
Philadelphia   New York

The author wishes to thank particularly Mrs. Janset Shami, Amman; Dr. Ibrahim Izzidin, Under-Secretary, Ministry of Culture and Information, Amman; and Mr. John Richardson, American Near East Refugee Aid, Washington, for locating many new photographs for this revised edition.

Ministry of Culture and Information: pp. 22, 43, 45, 50, 59, 62, 92, 100, 105, 111, 118, 120, 126, 127, 145, 150, 151

Ministry of Tourism and Antiquities: cover and pp. 12, 29, 33, 55, 56, 80, 88, 129

Jordan News Service: pp. 25, 133

Crystal, Amman: p. 112

Arab Development Society: pp. 16, 148

UNRWA: pp. 19, 83, 103, 132

Paul Copeland: pp. 37, 39, 111

U.S. Library of Congress Cataloging in Publication Data

Copeland, Paul W
  The land and people of Jordan.

(Portraits of the nations series)
  SUMMARY: An introduction to the geography, people, history, cities, and religions of Jordan, a constitutional monarchy in the Arab Middle East.
  1. Jordan—Juvenile literature. [1. Jordan] I. Stickles, Frances Copeland. II. Title.
DS153.C6 1972   915.695   72-5362
ISBN-0-397-31403-5

Map by Donald T. Pitcher

To MUSA BEY ALAMI with affection and admiration
for his unselfish work of making young refugees
useful citizens of Jordan

Contents

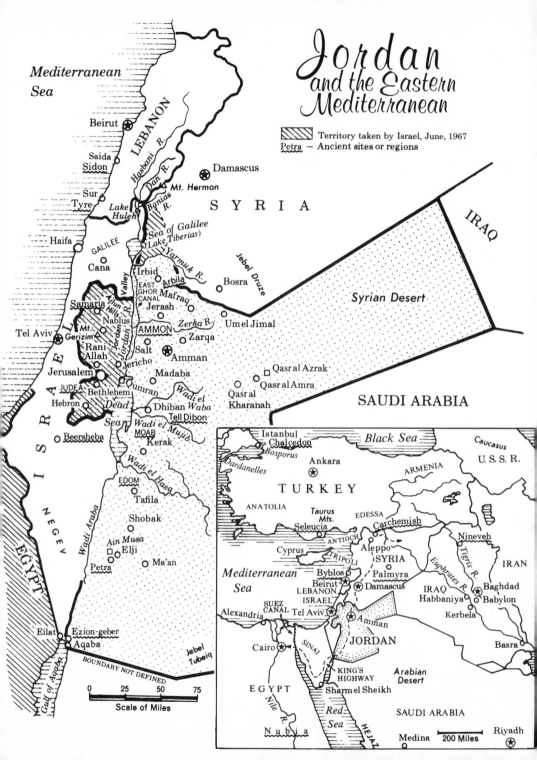

Jordan and the Eastern Mediterranean

Mediterranean Sea

⬚ Territory taken by Israel, June, 1967
Petra — Ancient sites or regions

Beirut

LEBANON

Saida
Sidon

Sur
Tyre

Haifa

Damascus

Mt. Hermon

Hasbani R.
Dan R.
Banias R.

Lake Huleh

Sea of Galilee (Lake Tiberias)

S Y R I A

GALILEE

Cana

Irbid

Arbila

Bosra

Jebel Druze

IRAQ

Syrian Desert

Yarmuk R.

EAST GHOR CANAL
Mafraq

Jerash

Zerka R.

Um el Jimal

Ajlun Hills

Samaria

Nablus

Mt. Gerizim

Tel Aviv

AMMON

Zarqa

Rani Allah

Jordan R.

Salt

Jericho

Amman

Jerusalem

JUDEA
Bethlehem

Madaba

Qumran

Qasr al Azrak

Qasr al Amra

Hebron

Dead Sea

Dhiban

Tell Dibon

Wadi el Waba

Qasr al Kharanah

SAUDI ARABIA

Beersheba

MOAB

Wadi el Mujib

Kerak

Wadi el Hasa

EDOM

Tafila

NEGEV

Wadi Araba

Shobak

EGYPT

Ain Musa
Elji

Petra

Ma'an

Gulf of Aqaba

Eilat

Ezion-geber

Aqaba

BOUNDARY NOT DEFINED

Jebel Tubeiq

0 25 50 75
Scale of Miles

Istanbul
Chalcedon

Bosporus

Black Sea

Caucasus

U. S. S. R.

Dardanelles

Ankara

ARMENIA

TURKEY

ANATOLIA

Taurus Mts.

EDESSA

Carchemish

Nineveh

Seleucia

ANTIOCH

Aleppo

Cyprus

TRIPOLI

SYRIA

IRAN

Mediterranean Sea

Byblos

Palmyra

Euphrates R.

Tigris R.

LEBANON

Beirut

Damascus

Baghdad

ISRAEL

IRAQ
Habbaniya

Babylon

SUEZ CANAL

Tel Aviv

Amman

Kerbela

Alexandria

JORDAN

Cairo

SINAI

Arabian Desert

Basra

EGYPT

KING'S HIGHWAY

SAUDI ARABIA

Nile R.

Sharm el Sheikh

Red Sea

HEJAZ

Nubia

Medina

200 Miles

Riyadh

1

Land of Contrasts

The Kingdom of Jordan is a fascinating collection of opposites. Politically it is very new yet very old. The ruins of its empires of antiquity are linked with modern highways. Its land contains mountains of eroded limestone and the deepest canyon in the world. Its climate ranges from the arid desert to the humid lushness of the Jericho oasis with its palms and acacias. Its temperature can change from the cold snowy hills of Jerusalem to the scorching heat of the southeastern desert. Its people are mostly Muslim but many of its shrines and sites are sacred also to Christian and Jewish pilgrims.

Jordan is also a country defined by military and political boundaries rather than those determined by physical features. Bounded on the north by Syria, on the east by Iraq, on the south by Saudi Arabia, and on the west by Israel, it lies in a strategic but often uncomfortable position in relation to its neighbors. Since June, 1967, the land west of the Jordan River, one-sixth of its territory, has been occupied by Israeli military forces. Except for a fifteen-mile coastline at Aqaba, its port on the Red Sea, the country is land-locked. Four-fifths of its 37,500 square miles, about the size of Indiana, is desert. This forces most of the over 2 million inhabitants to live in the northwestern sector of the country.

Perhaps on first sight the country seems bare, bland, and inhospitable. Longer acquaintance weaves a subtle enchantment. Jordan has the usual Mediterranean rainy season from November to March with the rest of the year hot and dry. At the beginning and the end of the dry season occurs the *khamsin,* a hot wind from the south and the southeast which blows steadily and oppressively, often causing dust storms. From June to September the *shamal* often blows from the north and northeast, causing extreme heat in the daytime but soothing cooler breezes after sundown. Rainfall is erratic and scattered. There is rarely enough to alter the surface of the land for soil renewal or for proper drainage and irrigation.

Jordan is split by a great gash in the earth's surface, the Great Rift that slashes from the Taurus Mountains of Turkey south to Tanzania in Africa. This great crack is deepest in the Jordan valley and the Dead Sea. The surface of the sea is 1,290 feet below sea level, the lowest place on the earth's surface, and the water is in some parts 1,200 feet deep. The half-mile depth of this rift is further accentuated by the hills paralleling it, which rise from 2,500 to 4,000 feet along the Jordan River, the Dead Sea, and the Wadi Araba to the south.

The main sources of the Jordan River begin at springs some 1,500 feet up the south side of Mount Hermon straddling the Lebanese-Syrian border. From there the river plunges precipitously to Lake Hulah only twelve miles south and then twelve more miles to the Sea of Galilee. In the short run of twenty-four miles the river has dropped 2,275 feet.

From there the river slowly twists its way south, meandering even more than the Turkish river, the Menderes, whose name gave us the adjective for excessive twisting or "meandering." The immediate banks are lined with sugarcane, tamarisk, and other rank brush which only emphasize the starkness of the hills on either side.

By the time the Jordan reaches the Dead Sea, the banks are barren and encrusted with salt. Nothing lives in the sea and no fishing boats bob on its surface. Except for its salinity and odor, little was actually known about the Dead Sea until 1848 when an American expedition headed by W. F. Lynch, a geologist, set out to explore the Rift. His party hauled two metal boats on cartwheels twenty-seven miles from the nearest coast, over the roadless hills of Galilee. Launching their boats on Lake Tiberias, they slowly drifted down the twisted channel of the Jordan to the Dead Sea. The only relief in the bleak landscape was the oasis of Jericho, small comfort in a vast glare of crystalline barrenness. There they spent twenty-two days crisscrossing the sea, taking soundings, and analyzing the water.

The Dead Sea is an inland lake with no outlet. The balance between the inflowing river and the rate of evaporation determines the salinity. The sea is 25 percent salty, seven times as salty as ocean water. Various soluble minerals compose this density and some of them are useful commercial resources.

As one flies into Jordan on a late afternoon when the shadows are lengthening, the land below reminds one of a huge pocket comb. The Great Rift forms the heavy back; the many big and little *wadis,* or dry riverbeds, that straggle in from the eastern desert are like gaping, twisted teeth. Most of these incised streamlines turn into rivers only in the rainy months of January and February. They are formidable barriers to travel at any time because the roads zigzag down and up their steep sides.

Beginning with the Yarmuk River on the northern border, the wadis, Arah Ziglad, el Yabis, Rajib, Zarqa, and Shukib, all empty into the depression of the Jordan River. The Wadi el Mujib and

Wadi Rum, a rugged and colorful area northeast of Aqaba, was used for many of the scenes in the film *Lawrence of Arabia*.

the Wadi el Hasa, opening into the middle and the lower end of the Dead Sea respectively, are truly awesome as one winds down and up their precipitous canyon walls. In the spring one is rewarded by a gorgeous display of oleander bushes along the drying riverbeds. Their vivid pinks and greens hearten one for the wearisome climb up to the next plateau.

In the north the Yarmuk River forms a natural boundary for some thirty miles. Another hundred miles of the border goes east through the boulder-strewn debris of the lava mountains of the Jebel Druze in Syria. From there on the boundary is one established by negotiations with the Saudi Arabians in 1965, adjusting an earlier boundary defined by the British. South of the Yarmuk, to the west, the rolling Ajlun hills are covered with orchards and patches of oak and pine. Speckled with clusters of the white square houses of the little villages, the hills roll west of the Jordan River in limestone ridges that are portions of ancient Samaria and Judea. The irregular western borders, hastily determined in 1949 by a United Nations commission along the battle positions held at the time the cease-fire was arranged between the Jews and the Arabs, contain familiar Biblical towns such as Nablus, Bethlehem, Hebron, and the Old City of Jerusalem. At the present time this part of Jordan is occupied territory and Amman's political control ends at the Jordan River.

Southward Jordan's western border is the Dead Sea and the Wadi Araba. Here the limestone hills of the north merge into outcroppings of sandstone. The hills become mountains that thrust their jagged outlines against the blue sky. Their palisaded ramparts, on closer view, show a variety of colors from gray to red which add beauty and interest to the fantastic shapes. The border reaches the sea at the head of the Gulf of Aqaba. From Aqaba the boundary extends eastward across the desert into a jumble of sandstone hills 150 miles in length, ending in the Jebel Tubeiq Mountains. Their sheer and forbidding cliffs hide narrow passes into the Saudi Arabian desert. Small pockets of garnets, turquoises, and amethysts are occasionally found in the maze of hidden valleys and secret caves.

The eastern border shared with Saudi Arabia was delimited by joint commissions which ran survey lines and built rock cairns. The nomadic Bedouin tribes pay little or no attention to such artificial barriers to their movements, sanctioned by centuries of grazing practices. Gently rolling hills form depressions in the flint-covered plain. These can become marshy lakes with sufficient rain and they attract the wandering tribesmen and their herds. The true desert contains a few wells and the large oasis of Azraq sixty miles east of Amman.

In a land so much of which is desert it is surprising to find such a variety of plants, most of them now familiar in our gardens. In April and early May, following the winter rains, the apparently dead and rocky desert blooms in unsuspected color. Diminutive but no less brilliant varieties of familiar flowers suddenly appear: scarlet anemones and tulips, wild orchids of many hues, blue cornflowers, yellow crowfoot like buttercups, field morning glories, yellow chrysanthemums that bloom in the spring, cyclamen ranging in colors from purple to white. There are blue lupin, pink flax, daisies, and iris, the ancestor of many of our hybrid irises. Anchusa, called *humhum* in Arabic, has tall stalks with flowers varying from blue to white. The leaves are good to eat, and are often used as poultices for men and animals. The pink cistus produces a fragrant oil called labdanum which is used in perfume.

Fragrant *ghadha* bushes ten to twelve feet high are a delicate-leaved cousin to our white and yellow broom. Gorse and other scrub bushes cover the hillsides. In the spring the desert is covered with a green fuzz of grass and the shallow depressions become meadows. In a few weeks this magic carpet disappears as mysteriously as it appeared and somber browns again cloak the land. The blue borage, a husky bush with blue, starlike, nodding flowers, has young leaves that taste like cucumber. The poplar willow, the tamarisk, and stunted pines are common trees, but overgrazing has caused erosion and few forests remain.

The two areas of forest that do remain are in the higher elevations of Ajlun and among the mountains near Ma'an in the south. These are areas of heavier rainfall, representing only 1 percent of the total land area. Olive trees, live oaks, Aleppo pines, hollies, and mastic trees are the forest regulars. Reforestation plans call for nine thousand acres of forest to be planted annually, including a program of tree planting in and around villages. The Turks denuded the hills of trees to keep the Hejaz railroad operating before World War I, and wars have taken their toll. But any for-

estry project demands a continual war with the goats, the greatest
enemy of young trees.

The animal life is fantastic when one considers the barren landscape. Hunters go after the ibex, somewhat similar to our mountain goat, and the gazelle, a very small deer, considering them
prime eating game. Next in preference are gray and ginger-col-
ored hares, larger than our familiar rabbits. The hyrax, sometimes called a rock-rabbit, is also good eating but is becoming
rare. Hyenas and jackals make the night discordant with their
quarreling and howling. Both are shot on sight since they attack
young lambs and also carry rabies. Wolves and wildcats are
hunted to preserve the game birds and the vineyards; both wolves
and foxes love grapes. Of the poisonous snakes, the Levant viper
is the most common. In the thickets south of the Dead Sea roam
wild boars. In the jagged mountains lynx, leopards, badgers, por-
cupines, and polecats are reported to live. How they subsist in
that jumble of rock is a marvel.

The amount of bird life is equally miraculous. Jordan is on one
of the migratory routes for birds, the most interesting of which
are the storks. It is quite a sight to find a familiar hillside covered
with gray boulders like large footballs. Then by some secret sig-
nal the footballs turn into storks, clumsily rising in flight on their
annual migration to nest in southern Turkey.

Tristan's grackle, found only around the Dead Sea, is much like
our familiar blackbird. More common are rock pigeons, wagtails,
thrushes, finches, swallows, tuneful warblers, and the fancy hoo-
poe with its fanlike head crest. Wild geese and ducks are plentiful, as are partridges, woodcocks, quail, grouse, and doves. Bus-
tards, looking like a cross between cranes and vultures, are as
good to eat as some of the other birds if one can ignore their ugly
appearance.

Although the land is barren it contains phosphates in sizable deposits. North of Amman and near Salt there are large beds of high quality and ninety miles south of Amman there is another deposit. The Dead Sea yields potash and various salts. Other minerals such as feldspar and gypsum are found in Jordan. Limestone for building and making cement is plentiful and there is sufficient marble to support several companies. Clay is made into sanitary pipe and bricks. No oil has been found but there is an oil refinery at Zarqa which has reduced the cost of petroleum products within Jordan.

The land is sharply divided between the desert and portions with resources, soil to support farming and pastures, and the water for town life. A small proportion of the population lives in the vast desert and the bulk lives in the small portion of the country where agricultural and urban life is possible.

Jordan River valley farming depends on irrigation and land reclamation.

2

Pleasant People

The Kingdom of Jordan is unique in having a homogeneous population, more than 90 percent of whom are Arabs of the Muslim faith. Almost two-thirds of the population is twenty years of age or younger and there are slightly more women than men.

Ninety percent of the Jordanian population lives on only 15 percent of the land area. Urban and rural groups of the population are almost equally divided and no more than 5 percent are true nomads, breeding camels and living a self-sufficient life on their meat, milk, hair, skin, and dung. Those living in rural areas cluster in villages of between four hundred and eight hundred inhabitants. Most of them raise small crops, although some are traders, miners, or craftsmen.

The only large group of foreign origin are the Circassian refugees from the Caucasus. They are refugees from a Czarist Russian persecution in 1870. The Turkish caliph, Abdul Hamid, settled them in and around Amman to act as a buffer between the raiding desert tribes and the agricultural villages. Further waves of immigration continued for a number of years. They are Muslims in faith, have been easily accepted by their Arab neighbors, and still wear their distinctive long black coats and conical wool caps.

Jordanians trace their Arabism to the seventh century when the indigenous people were conquered by Muslim tribes. The invaders brought their language, Arabic, their religion, and their traditions and since that time the inhabitants have been called Arabs. Other tribes had conquered the area at earlier periods, including the Hebrews, but their influence was brief and did not affect a large area. After the Roman persecutions the Hebrews left Palestine and Jordan. The people who remained behind continued to speak Aramaic but they were Christians. It was easy for them to assimilate another Semitic influence when the Arabs came.

Arabic is a rhythmic language, full of poetic expressions, and with colloquial variations even within the country. It is a language shared by Arabs in other countries and, because the Koran is written in Arabic, the language binds Jordanian Muslims in worship with all the Muslim countries. Jordan has postal and telephone service throughout the Kingdom and national radio and television stations. Arabic is the official language for these services, but many Jordanians are also familiar with Armenian, Kurdish, Greek, Hebrew, Turkish, or English.

Physically the Jordanians are slender of build with medium to short stature and dark complexions. Thin faces with dark brown eyes are framed by dark brown or black hair. People living west of the Jordan River are inclined to be taller, broader, and less sharp-featured.

One-third of Jordan's 2 million plus inhabitants are Palestinians. They are Muslim Arabs, part of whose country, Palestine, was lost to them through a United Nations decision in 1947, followed by further losses in the 1948 war with Israel. The United Nations plan of partition gave most of the fertile, urban coast to Israel and the hinterland to the Palestinians. Many Palestinians who found themselves in the Israeli sections at the time of partition fled into the area east of Jerusalem, expecting to return when the fighting stopped. In the nightmare of events following a cease-fire negotiated by the United Nations, the Palestinians were cut off from their homes, businesses, and livelihood. They were not allowed to return nor were they compensated. There was no plan in the Partition Agreement for moving residents from one section to another. The Palestinians were overnight refugees in sight of their homes and homeland.

The largest number of refugees camped around Hebron and Jericho, which eventually became organized communities waiting for a future. The United Nations Relief and Works Agency (UNRWA) managed their food and housing and provided medical, sanitary, and educational services as funds allowed. In 1950 Jordan annexed what was left of Palestine after a vote to do so by

Palestinian women learn dressmaking in a UNRWA school for refugees.

the Palestinians themselves. The Palestinians are full citizens of Jordan, but they also represent a tremendous economic problem to the young country.

UNRWA has continued its services, year after year. At present 250,000 of the original 700,000 needing assistance still remain on the West Bank. The others crossed the river into east Jordan, along with 100,000 other people, after the 1967 war with Israel. Those Jordanians remaining on the West Bank are in limbo. They have family and national ties with Jordan, but officially they are restricted by their Israeli military rulers.

Jordan is divided into eight administrative subdivisions called *liwas*. Each is centered around one of the country's main towns: Kerak, Ma'an, Amman, Nablus, Irbid, Jerusalem, Hebron, or Balqa. They are the traditional centers of government, commerce, finance, light industry, and the services of schools and hospitals. The towns and villages are organized with an elected leader, the *muhktar* or headman. This man is the link between the village and the government. He represents all the inhabitants including farmers, craftsmen, shopkeepers, teachers, and shepherds.

The Bedouins, who were the larger part of Jordan's population before 1948, are now more settled and less of a romantic legend. Gradually the tribes are accepting an agricultural life, because it is more economically rewarding. Black tents on the desert may be good dwellings in the warm spring air; but tents are far from comfortable in the bitter cold of winter or the scorching dust-laden winds of summer.

The tents are usually made of a heavy black goat-hair felt, in strips eighteen to twenty-four inches wide. The tribesmen pace off the strips in the markets, haggling over the price. Rolled up, the strips are easily transported on camels while a tent of military canvas would be a bulky, cumbersome object to move. The strips are laced together with thread or are fastened together by wooden pegs.

One quickly learns to gauge the social importance of an encampment of Bedouins by the number of poles supporting the main tent which always faces east. If there are five poles the tent may be as big as ninety by thirty feet and the owner is undoubtedly a sheik of great importance. Tents of two or three poles are more common. Every tent is divided by a curtain, the *riwaq*, to separate the women's quarters, or *hareem*, from the men's quarters, or *muksaad*.

If danger threatens, the tents tightly cluster like the traditional wagon train of the Old West. Otherwise the tents will be scattered in clusters over great distances in order to facilitate the grazing of herds. With big tribes like the Beni Sakhr, numbering around fifteen thousand, the tents will be in clusters of forty to fifty spread over an area of five or more miles.

On the perimeter of a large encampment of black tents are one or more brown tents. They house the members of the Sani tribe who are experts in blacksmithing; they are artisans who repair guns, shoe horses, and make swords. Other brown tents shelter the Sleybs, a tribe with blue eyes and red or blond hair. They are much like gypsies in temperament, are entertainers and traders between desert and town. They are also famous for the white donkeys they breed.

All tribes and subtribes, even those who are reduced to one family, are headed by a sheik, meaning literally "gray beard," who in practice is the wise elder. He is advised by a council of elders or, in larger groups, by other sheiks. The ruling sheik holds his position by his astute management of tribal affairs, his wise judgments in disputes, and his personal qualities as a popular leader. The office is not necessarily hereditary but is subject to tribal de-

Bedouin boys lead settled lives while they attend government schools.

cision. Often, however, the sheik's favorite son is given superior education and training in administration by attending tribal councils, so that he is usually the obvious choice.

The Bedouin tribes are divided into two large groups. Those in the north, such as the large Luwal tribe, take traditional pride in being descendants of Ishmael, son of Abraham and his Egyptian wife, Hagar. In the south the tribes, like the Beni Sakhr and Taamirah, are equally proud to claim descent from the Biblical *Yoktan,* ancestor of the Yemeni tribes of southern Arabia.

The Jordanian Bedouins graze east and west, but the Ruallah, some of whom tent in Syria, graze southward into Saudi Arabia, a trek of over five hundred miles. This cross-pattern of migrations offers opportunities for clashes, raids, and petty wars. Like Syria and Iraq, the Jordanian government has been trying to settle the tribes and has partially succeeded with the Taamirah who have settled down in the eastern valley of the Dead Sea and live in houses at least part of the year.

As an incentive to adopting more permanent settlements and as a deterrent to tribal warfare, the government has allocated areas of land, dug wells, and built herringbone patterns of low stone dams in the smaller wadis to hold back the spring freshets and increase the growth of grass. It also provides young fruit trees, seed for crops, and technicians to help the would-be farmers get started. It is a slow process to change the habits of millennia. While not giving up his herds, the Bedouin is smart enough to see the advantage of having a second source of food against the years when rainfall does not come in time to produce grass.

The Bedouin feast of roast lamb stuffed with rice, highly spiced with cinnamon, called *mansaf,* served with yogurt, has become a national dish. It is both a restaurant specialty and a desert ceremony to serve this meal. A favorite on the West Bank is *musakham,* chicken steamed in olive oil sauce with onion and sumac. In Jerusalem a "speciality of the city" is *maqlouba,* a stewlike dish of vegetables, including eggplant or cauliflower and meat served on rice. In Hebron the favorite dinner is *kidreh bil-Furn* which is an oven-baked stew of meat, rice, chickpeas, and spices. For those who prefer, there is *Daud Pasha,* a stew of meatballs, whole onions, and pine nuts cooked with tomatoes and served with rice, or *bateenjan battiri,* eggplant stuffed with meat and rice cooked in tomato sauce. There are many finely chopped salads in the Jordanian cuisine and several sweet cakes of paper-thin pastry filled with white cheese, walnuts, or pistachios and served with honey or a sugar syrup. Apricots, melons, avocados, guavas, and figs are enjoyed in season as well as oranges from the groves that have flourished in the Jericho valley for centuries. Each family in olive country is sure its centuries-old recipe for pickling olives is superior to that of its neighbors. Beer and wine, both red and white, are brewed and bottled in Jordan and are considered aids to digestion by Muslims who consider moderation rather than abstinence the intention of religious rules.

Jordanians are traditionally farmers. Some own their land, others lease state-owned land. In other instances the villagers own all the land as a community and share the crops. Islam encouraged the growth of towns as the place for the mosque and the religious school. These and other services are shared by villagers today. Village life encourages oral communication, which is particularly important for those who have more faith in traditional sayings than in facts printed in newspapers and books. The coffeehouse, the village market, the mosque courtyard, and even the cemetery are meeting places for villagers. Increasingly Bedouins go to towns to barter for things they cannot provide for themselves. As they exchange news they have a tenuous contact with the country at large.

The towns and villages of Jordan cling to the hilltops as much as possible to enjoy what breezes there are and to save every square inch of land for cultivation. Most of the houses are built of the native lime or sandstone, boxlike in form and usually white-washed on the outside as well as inside. Simple wooden furniture, a bed with rope webbing, straight chairs, and a cupboard or two, is sufficient. In the poorer homes, quilts spread on the floor over reed mats provide the family beds. People living in the villages dress more traditionally in the clothing best adapted to the climate. The free-flowing gown, the *galibiyah,* or the baggy trousers, called *sherwal,* of the artisan, do not restrict movement or cling to the body. The head scarf, *kafiyah,* held on by a black cord, or *agal,* protects the neck and shoulders, shades the eyes, and can be drawn across the mouth and nose in case of a dust storm.

Many Palestinian village women still preserve their traditionally beautiful, festive dresses. Sections of a given dress were handed down from mother to daughter for several generations, to be sewed into the new version of the dress as repairs or alterations were necessary. Each village or region was known for its own dis-

Folk dancers, wearing traditional clothes, practice in Jerash for a festival.

tinctive patterns, usually done in cross-stitch. Because of its particular beauty the Bethlehem dress was often commissioned as a wedding dress by other townswomen, and embroiderers in Bethlehem supplied panels of the Bethlehem dress to order. The embroidery in cotton and silk threads shows brightly against the indigo-dyed cotton homespun and brightened any special occasion. Fine collections of these historic marvels of needlework may be found in the Palestine Archeological Museum and in private collections in Amman.

As in many other countries, old ways are rapidly being replaced by less distinctive new ones as the world is brought together by films, transistor radios, and television. In Amman, where half a million Jordanians live, people dress in the mass-produced trousers, shirts, and dresses of Europe and America. Their homes are furnished in locally-made versions of European and American furniture. Amman boasts the largest variety of shopping in Jordan and is the gateway to the rest of the world. From its airport one can fly by Royal Jordan Airline, *Alia,* named after the king's first child, to other parts of the Middle East and to Europe. Other international airlines link Jordan with farther distant points, and eight other airports link other Jordanian towns to Amman. There is also a good network of roads and main highways north and south on each side of the Jordan River. The main highway south leads to Aqaba; the main highway north splits to go either to Syria or to Iraq. Bridges across the Jordan River lead to Jerusalem and to Nablus. A narrow-gauge railroad passes through Amman on its journey from Ma'an to Damascus. Amman is the hub, a true center for the Jordanian people.

3

The Open-Air Museum

The cities of Jordan offer an open-air history book and museum that is rivaled by very few countries. The layers of human life are many, offering glimpses into a variety of life patterns, passions, and beliefs. Basically all of these forebears to the land that is now Jordan struggled with the same basic environment, a fertile valley threatened by a desert. These forebears also found themselves frequently at the mercy of invaders because they were "in the way" or "right on the road" or "in the center of things." King Hussein I of Jordan is very aware of this heritage and his duties as custodian to it. So is Jordan's Department of Antiquities which has done, and continues to do, a good job of discovering, preserving, and restoring this storehouse of historical information.

JERICHO

Palestine is one of the places where man made his first attempts at cultivating wild grains and domesticating wild animals. By 4000 B.C. Palestinians knew a settled community life. Then their neighbors in Egypt and Mesopotamia accelerated their development. They reached out in war and trade along their rivers and across the land bridge of Jordan between them.

The interplay of these cultures was considerable and often disrupting. At the same time many tribes came into the Jordan valley from Arabia, Hebrew and Arab tribes among them. They came to raid and they stayed to grow crops, live in towns, and give new lifeblood to the indigenous people. Their history, despite the Bible, is not nearly as well known as their neighbors' because Egyptian and Mesopotamian written records extend much further back in history. The inhabitants of the Jordan valley invented no calendar, either, because they did not depend on annual flooding, as along the Nile, for irrigation.

Jericho, twenty-two miles northeast of Jerusalem, is built in an oasis fed by a perennial spring. It provides one thousand gallons of precious water a minute which can sustain a lush vegetation of palm trees and banana groves. Behind the town rises the massive Mount of Temptation. The ancient town and the modern town sit side by side at the present time. This made it possible for Kathleen Kenyon, a British archeologist, to direct an extensive excavation of the ancient site.

She found a walled community for two thousand inhabitants, occupied about 8000 B.C. Up to that time the people around Jericho had been hunters living in caves. The men sharpened their hard stone scrapers, chisels, and knives on coarse stones. The women learned to spin and weave animal fibers, to plait rushes into baskets, and to harden clay pots by firing them. At first the copious spring was merely a convenient place to hunt thirsty animals who came to drink. Later, men learned to corral and tame such useful animals as sheep, goats, and cattle. Gradually the idea of a permanent community took shape in men's minds.

They built a compact village of houses made of sun-dried brick much as they are built today. (Before 3000 B.C. the bricks were shaped like oval loaves of bread; since then they have been formed in flat wooden molds.) Around the town a heavy wall surrounded a ditch. Against one wall a tower of stone and mortar rose at least to the present thirty-foot height. On one side a protected staircase led from a room on the top of the tower, obviously for defense and observation.

There were many clues to life in early Jericho. The large number of animal bones suggests that animals watering at the spring were either trapped or domesticated for food. The presence among the artifacts of more flint sickles than arrowheads implies an agricultural rather than a hunting community. The discovery of irrigation ditches adds further evidence.

The archeologist's most valuable aids in dating sites are pot-

The excavation site at Jericho is shadowed by the Mount of Temptation.

sherds, broken bits of pottery which will survive indefinitely in a dry climate. A table of shapes and styles, textures and glazes, has been devised to give a working timetable for the strata in which they are found. This is particularly important in an area where written records do not exist. A second aid to dating antiquities is the recently developed method called "carbon 14." This is a naturally radioactive isotope of carbon with an atomic mass of 14 and a half-life of 5,700 years. It is used in dating carbon-containing objects such as wood, grains, or bone. For very ancient sites this is a particularly valuable tool and makes it possible to say that Jericho is 10,000 years old.

The town flourished until it was destroyed by fire about 1590 B.C. The later political history is not such a tranquil picture. The Old Testament records fairly accurately the murder, treachery, palace intrigues, and massacres that occurred among the petty states and shifting alliances. The aggressive Hebrew tribes finally established two kingdoms west of the Jordan River, and then under King Solomon merged them into an empire occupying both sides of the river and south to Aqaba.

The aromatic balsam bushes that grow in this area are said to be descendants of seed brought by the Queen of Sheba to King Solomon. Many centuries later another queen, Cleopatra, charmed Roman Marc Antony into giving her the Jordanian and coastal cities as a personal gift. Cleopatra took balsam cuttings to a herbal garden near Heliopolis and gardeners to tend the unusual plants.

Rebellions following Solomon's death opened the way for a Syrian invasion from the north, and an Egyptian raid on Jerusalem looted the treasures of Solomon. The discord made it relatively easy for the powerful Assyrians to attack Damascus and after a two-year siege to capture it in 732 B.C. The Assyrians then swept south and added Palestine to their provinces. Ten years later Sargon II marched most of the rebellious population off to Baby-lonia as captives. In their place Sargon settled some of his veter-ans but colonization failed to discourage revolts. In 701 B.C. Sennacherib chastised forty-six fortified towns and collected all the royal treasure.

The power of Assyria waned. The Medes and Scythians from the north and the Babylonians from the south converged on Nin-eveh, and the Assyrian capital fell in 612 B.C. Nebuchadnezzar defeated the Egyptians in their attempt to fill the power vacuum in Jordan. He marched on Jerusalem to collect its treasure and, rounding up the priests, princes, and other high officials, carried them off in chains to Babylon. Nebuchadnezzar returned to Jor-dan after another revolt and burned the major fortified towns and besieged Jerusalem. It fell in 586 B.C. The defeated King Zede-kiah was blinded and he and all able-bodied people west of the Jordan River were rounded up and driven off to Babylon.

While wars were being fought across this territory, trade was continuing. East of the Jordan River lay the ancient King's High-way, the caravan route between Egypt and the eastern empires. The route crossed the Sinai Peninsula to the head of the Gulf of Aqaba, then threaded its way north through the foothills, follow-ing the natural springs to Damascus, Aleppo, and on to the Eu-phrates River. The Egyptians worked copper and turquoise mines along the route in Sinai. Solomon opened copper mines and built smelters near present-day Aqaba. The blast furnaces were designed to make use of the strong winds whipping down the Wadi Araba. They provided Solomon with copper and iron ingots for trade.

The movement of commodities during the years 1500 B.C. to 1000 B.C. was astonishingly varied. Cyprus exported copper; Lebanon, cedar wood; Egypt, papyrus and textiles; Nubia, ivory and gold. Asia Minor traded silver and cattle. Syria produced wines, chariots, and women's hairpins. Rare woods and incense came from Arabia; fine textiles and metalwork were imported from India. Jericho was in a key position to profit by this ebb and flow of trade, to the envy of her neighbors. Jericho, with strong defensive walls and towers, was the pivotal town between nomadic desert tribes and frugal farming communities. Others controlled the caravans and regulated the flow of goods.

PETRA

The city of Petra, Biblical *Selah,* the rock, was a hidden valley stronghold in the awesome mountains of southern Jordan. This part of Jordan, east of the Dead Sea, was taken over from the original inhabitants by Esau and his large family, servants, flocks, and herds. Esau was the son of Isaac who was tricked out of his inheritance by his twin brother, Jacob.

Angered and embittered, Esau moved to the eastern side of the Wadi Araba called Edom. A bitter feud resulted that lasted for centuries. One important result was that Moses' request for passage through Edom, on his way to the "promised land," was denied by the Edomites. The account of almost continuous warfare between Esau's descendants and the people of Judah and Israel can be found in the Old Testament books of Judges, Samuel, and Kings.

Toward the end of the eighth century B.C., the Edomites were either dispersed or absorbed by the Arabs of the desert. The Nabateans, as this new people came to be called, took over the caravan route of the King's Highway through Edom. They raided the caravans and then disappeared into the rugged sandstone mountains to hide their treasure in a hidden valley. After the conquest of the eastern world by Alexander the Great, his generals divided up the conquered lands upon his death in 323 B.C. Their greed

The entrance to Petra through the *siq* frames the so-called Treasury of the Nabateans.

led to more than two centuries of constant warfare over the riches of the area.

In the third century B.C. a Seleucid army from the north made a raid on the Nabateans. Their treasure was captured, but the Nabatean men, who had been away at a conference, rallied and tracked the raiders to their camp. Through carelessness and over-confidence the Greeks had posted no guards. The Nabateans fell on the camp, killed most of the army of four thousand, and recovered their treasure as well as other plunder in the camp.

This experience taught the Nabateans that it might be more

profitable to set up, for a price, an armed convoy system guaranteeing the caravans' safe transit through Jordan than to continue their robber policy. This is the earliest known insurance organization and it paid well for several centuries. They also moved into the hidden valley of Petra, which enhanced their security.

Under this new system the Nabateans grew rich. Commercial operations were carried on at Wadi Musa, outside the hidden valley, a village by a never-failing spring. Tradition calls it the spring of Moses but that spring is more accurately identified in southern Sinai. There was no need for the caravan leaders to learn of the secret entrance to the hidden city. Trade flourished and Petra's citizens grew wealthy.

By the end of the second century B.C., the Nabateans were organized as a powerful kingdom. King Obodas I, about 90 B.C., was strong enough to defeat Alexander Jannaeus, the Roman governor of Palestine, and unite the whole country east of the Jordan River. His son Aretas III extended the kingdom northward to include Damascus.

The Roman general Pompey sent an army against Petra but the citizens bought it off. About 40 B.C., however, the Romans defeated the Nabateans and forced them to pay an annual tribute as a Roman ally. Later Marc Antony gave a large part of Arabia, including Nabatea, to Cleopatra, who then collected the tribute. King Malchus II was slow in his payments to Cleopatra so she plotted with Herod the Great, governor of Palestine, to help her collect. The first attempt failed but, in 31 B.C. with Cleopatra and Antony dead, Herod succeeded in annexing the northern part of Jordan.

The Roman world became an empire under Augustus Caesar. He started reorganizing the provinces and sent an army to invade and subdue Arabia. Obodas III, the Nabatean king from 28 to 9

B.C., who had no love for Rome, offered his chief minister, Sylla-cus, as a guide to lead the Romans across the Arabian desert. The latter led the army by the most waterless route and great numbers of the soldiers died of thirst.

Aretas IV ruled from 9 B.C. to A.D. 40 in comparative peace ex-cept for a quarrel with Herod Antipas, then Roman governor of Palestine. The latter had married Aretas's daughter but now wanted to get rid of her in order to marry his brother's wife, He-rodias, mother of Salome. It was Herodias who persuaded Salome to ask for the head of John the Baptist because he had criticized the marriage. Aretas attacked and defeated Herod Antipas. He was saved from Roman vengeance by the fortuitous death of the Emperor Tiberius.

Little more is known of Petra after the last king, Rabel II, died in A.D. 106. In that year the Nabatean lands were incorporated into the Roman province of Arabia, and the administrative capi-tal was established at Bosra in modern Syria. The century before and the one after the birth of Christ were the Nabateans' golden years. The Romans, with characteristic zeal, built roads, temples, and a theater in Petra, all of which remain today.

Time moved on and in the third century caravan traffic along the edge of the desert started to fade away. Trade was being di-verted to merchant ships in the Red Sea as being safer and quicker than the camel caravans. In the north an Arab kingdom at Palmyra was diverting caravans to the Euphrates River, form-ing a new east-west pattern of trade. By the seventh century when the Muslim invasion swept over the land, Petra had become a for-gotten city, a ghost town lost in the mountains of Edom.

In 1812 the intrepid, not to say foolhardy, Swiss explorer, John Lewis Burkhardt, rediscovered Petra. Disguised as an Arab pil-grim, he succeeded in getting a local guide to take him into the city on the pretext that he had made a holy vow to make a sacrifice at the tomb of Aaron which is supposed to be on Mount Hor overlooking Petra. He made his sacrifice at the foot of the mountain and got out quickly, because the guide was suspicious and threatened to kill him.

During the nineteenth century a handful of brave souls ventured to visit Petra but it was not until the early twentieth century that a few wealthy tourists made the trip from Jerusalem. The caravans, heavily armed and escorted by Turkish soldiers, could make the trip to Petra and return in a month.

After World War I the British army built a road from the railway town of Ma'an, 130 miles south of Amman as the crow flies, to Elji, the modern town outside the mountain walls of Petra. The citizens of the adjacent village of Wadi Musa, fearing the road would rob them of their pitifully small business of renting horses to visitors, resisted fiercely. In fact, the first garrison of the Arab Legion post at Elji was massacred. After the rebellion was crushed, the government agreed not to put a road into Petra.

In 1961 a team of archeologists sponsored by a number of American institutions did extensive work toward repairing the quake-shattered theater. The stage was excavated and walls and decorative statuary were replaced. The following year scholars gathered under government sponsorship to commemorate the 150th anniversary of the rediscovery of Petra.

Even today it is not an easy trip. Cars are left at Elji, and visitors and luggage are transferred to the backs of scrawny horses. Setting out in single file in the cool of the evening, each horse is led by an Arab youth singing to frighten away evil spirits. The path is strewn with boulders continually rearranged by winter torrents, and the entrance to the hidden city is through a vertical-walled cleft called the *Siq*. This crack in the walls of the mountain range twists and turns for well over a mile and hides the stars above by its narrowness. Neither horse nor rider can an-

Tomb chambers at Petra, elaborate and simple, dot the cliff surface.

ticipate where the next slide of stones lies. Finally more level ground is reached, the stars gleam above vague towering crags, and lights shine in the distance. The eerie ride ends with the promise of a camp supper and a cot in a cave or tent.

The cave houses, tombs, and monuments, over one thousand of them, are cut into the red-brown sandstone streaked with rose, blue, orange, gray, and green. The facades are carved in a variety of styles, blended by the Nabateans from Greek, Roman, and Assyrian influences into a distinctive style of their own. The craftsmen started at the top, carving down the face of the cliff. They carved deep enough into the stone to provide a two-foot-wide shelf of rock that made a scaffold as they worked their way to ground level.

When the Nabateans decided to build homes in their treasure-house valley, they needed water. The average annual rainfall in the region is only five inches, and there are few springs. The Nabateans devised methods for leading the water off bare plateaus into cisterns cut in the narrow rocky valleys. They cut channels in the rock to lead water into the city and even into the buildings. If rock-cut conduits weren't enough, they fashioned plastered pottery pipes. In order to prevent water rushing through the Siq, where it was not wanted, they built a dam near the entrance to divert occasional cloudbursts into a tunnel and a walled trench. The water was guided around the perimeter of Petra and into a wider valley.

Most of Petra was carved out of living rock; only the freestanding buildings have suffered from earthquakes. The leveled mountaintop where they worshipped still has its raised stone altar with a drain to carry off the blood from sacrificial animals. The Nabatean's language was a form of Aramaic with Arabic influences; their script evolved into Kufic, an angular form of Arabic. The Nabateans, however, were better at tallying their commercial accounts than at recording their own history. They were also superb hydraulic engineers. Little is known of their life-style beyond these outlines. Their importance waned as imperial Rome grew.

JERASH

The Roman conqueror Pompey included Jerash in the new province of Syria in 63 B.C and built it into an important frontier city. Inscriptions found there indicate that the original mud hut village was enlarged by the Greek king of Egypt, Ptolemy II, about the time he changed the village of Amman into the city of Philadelphia. True to the Roman colonial practice, Jerash was allowed a great deal of religious and administrative independence. Jerash was one of the first ten cities of the area to federate loosely in a commercial union, referred to as the Decapolis. Trade was the chief objective, an early example of today's "common market." Through this league Jerash had trade connections with the Nabateans, and several temples were dedicated to Nabatean gods.

Thanks to the wealth accumulated through trade, a master plan for the "city beautiful" was approved in the middle of the first century A.D. Jerash was renewed in the best Roman fashion, as may be seen today. There was a long, narrow hippodrome for athletic contests and chariot racing. Lower in the valley was an oval-shaped forum paved with stone and lined with an impressive colonnade; more than half of the columns still stand. The grand avenue was once flanked on either side by 260 columns linked by an entablature on top.

The forum of Roman Jerash overlooks the present-day town in the valley.

The eastern half of Jerash follows the slope of the hillside to the river where modern Jerash is located. The western half of the city covers a gently rising hill. A temple dedicated to the Roman goddess Diana stood large on the hill with its florid Corinthian columns forty-five feet tall. The columned streets, the baths and other public buildings, the temples, all combine to show what a Roman provincial city was like. The business and residential area stretching toward the river is not preserved but the pattern of streets and grand stairways is evident from the preservation on the other side of the grand avenue.

Jerash prospered under Roman rule. When Trajan extended the imperial frontiers, the southern kingdom of Nabatea was included. In the winter of A.D. 129–130 a triumphal arch was erected to honor a visit from the Emperor Hadrian. New roads laced the empire together and Jerash, like many cities, benefited from the augmented volume of trade. Earlier buildings were torn down and built again in a more resplendent style. Citizens vied with each other in donating monuments, altars, pedestals, and statues, and in subsidizing festivals and athletic contests. One inscription praises the munificence of Titus Flavius Quirina who became famous for his banquets to both winning and losing contestants.

Roman influence reached its peak early in the third century and waned as external pressures began to constrict the Imperial borders. The barbarians were pressing and the Roman legions withdrew to re-form behind the barrier of the Danube River. The Persians overran eastern Asia Minor. At Palmyra, on the Syrian desert, the Emperor Aurelian fought the Persians and dragged the independent Queen Zenobia off to Rome in chains. The city was sacked and its destruction broke the commercial link between East and West for a time. Jerash was one of the first frontier cities to feel the effect.

The power base in the Roman Empire shifted to present-day Istanbul, the headquarters of the Emperor Constantine. In 312 he saw a cross in the sky and the written phrase meaning "by this sign will you conquer." The vision convinced him that only under the Christian cross would he be victorious. Constantine became sole ruler of the crumbling Roman Empire. He proclaimed Christianity the state religion and the ancient city of Byzantium was renamed Constantinople.

Jerash revived as a flourishing center of Christian worship. By the middle of the fourth century a cathedral had been built at street level outside the gate to the temple of Diana. On the hillside above, a courtyard contained a fountain whose legendary water changed into wine on the anniversary of the miracle at Cana. On the strength of this wonder, pious visitors were attracted and Jerash prospered.

Inscriptions indicate that Bishop Exeresius represented Jerash in the Council at Seleucia in 359, and that the city was represented by Bishop Plancus at the Council of Chalcedon in 451. Obviously by that time it was a strong Christian center. In the fifth century the Church of the Apostles, Prophets, and Martyrs was built near the north gate on the lower slope of the hill. Back of the cathedral and farther up the hill, another church was built to the memory of St. Theodore. Under the Emperor Justinian's rule, seven more churches were built. These churches collapsed because of shoddy construction, sometimes assisted by earthquakes. Careless craftsmen often used materials from earlier buildings, hiding what they did with luxurious facings of marble. Even the jewelry of that era reflects a false prosperity; the earrings were gold-plated bronze and the ostentatious jewels were glass.

The empire was crumbling, too. The Persians had been raiding the borders of Armenia and Syria for nearly four hundred years.

They finally broke through the weak Byzantine defenses, and in Jerash two goal posts remain in the hippodrome to recall the Persian love of polo. In 614 the Persians captured Damascus and sacked Jerusalem. Amidst the booty carried away by the conquerors was the "true cross" that Queen Helena, the mother of Constantine, had found three centuries earlier. The Byzantine Emperor Heraclius, in a successful campaign against the Persians, recovered the cross in September, 629, and returned it to Jerusalem. During the tumultuous welcome he received there, he was too busy to notice dispatches. One told of a strong Arab raid out of the southern desert, the prelude to the Muslim conquest which began four years later.

QUMRAN

One of the great true mystery stories of the twentieth century is set in a hot and dusty wadi disgorging into the western bank of the Dead Sea. There a young Arab herdsman, while hunting a missing goat, stopped to wipe his sweaty face. It was the summer of 1947. He noticed a cave opening nearby and threw a stone into it. Instead of the usual "baa"—herders direct their flocks by throwing stones with remarkable accuracy—he heard something shatter. Naturally the boy did not enter the cave because, as everyone knows, evil spirits are often confined in jars. Next day, with the moral support of a young companion, he entered the cave and found some tall pottery jars, most of them empty. One contained a roll of leather wrapped in rags. This the boys took to their tent, unrolled it, and discovered there was writing on it. Instead of cutting it up for shoe leather, they saved it.

Two years later it appeared on the antique market in Jerusalem. It proved to be the earliest known edition of the Book of Isaiah. An expedition under G. Lankester Harding, then Director of Antiquities, searched the area and investigated almost forty caves. Other scholars and archeologists joined the search, and many tribesmen, particularly the Taamireh, and shepherds hunted for other treasure-filled caves.

All told, some two hundred caves have been explored in the region of this first find at Qumran, and twelve of them have yielded scrolls and fragments of documents and manuscripts. Many of them were in poor condition because they had not been stored in jars or had suffered other misfortunes from men, animals, and weather through the centuries. The caves in which they were found, however, probably represent the least changed habitations dating from the time of Jesus.

Six seasons of excavation during the 1950's at the community center at Qumran have established the history of the desert community. The spot was apparently used originally as a fort during the seventh century B.C. In the second century B.C., an unorthodox group of Jews, called the Essenes, disagreed with the ruling

Wadi Qumran, with its many caves, yielded the treasured Essene scrolls.

priestly group in Jerusalem, the Maccabees, and fled to Qumran. They continued their separate existence for two centuries, farming and herding, studying the Scripture, worshipping and praying for their way to triumph over the wicked priests in Jerusalem.

A violent earthquake in the spring of 31 B.C. split the town in two, dropping the eastern half by three and a half feet. The Essenes did not rebuild for twenty-five years but the new town boasted a flour mill and bake shop, pottery kilns, grain storage bins, and furnaces for smelting metal. All was prosperous and peaceful until the Roman occupation of Palestine provoked an uprising in A.D. 66. The Essenes sided with other rebellious Jewish groups. Within the next two years the settlement of Qumran was occupied by the Tenth Legion from Jericho and the inhabitants were massacred.

The community of Qumran, like most archeological digs, is a disappointing complex of mud-brick and stone foundations offering little to be dramatized by the camera. Careful inspection does show a well-planned arrangement of kitchen, dining room, library, storerooms, and dormitories. The only unusual feature was an ingenious system of cisterns. Evidently there were three or four degrees of sanctity among the Essenes. Those of lower rank were not permitted to pollute the pool of the next higher order by bathing in it.

South of Qumran documents were found in caves near Hebron. Most of them belonged to fugitives from a first-century A.D. revolt against the Romans, but a seventh-century B.C. Hebrew papyrus was also in the cache. In caves north of Masada, still in the wilderness district of Judah, documents in Nabatean, Greek, and Aramaic were found in a Byzantine monastery. Eight miles north of Jericho some of the earliest papyri were found in cliffs of the Jordan fault. The documents, of which only fragments were found, are in Aramaic and on legal subjects. They were taken to the cave

The fragments of the Dead Sea Scrolls have been painstakingly pieced together, studied, and preserved.

by Samaritans who died there, perhaps after fleeing Alexander the Great's soldiers in 331 B.C.

Scholars will be many years piecing together the various fragments and completing their translations. The fragments themselves turned up over a period of fifteen years, and more might turn up in the future. Enough work has been done to establish the fact that the manuscripts are the earliest sources of Old Testament chapters known today. Until these discoveries, the oldest Hebrew source for the Bible dated from the ninth century. The Dead Sea Scrolls span a period from the seventh century B.C. to the second century A.D. Thanks to the Essenes and all the others who wrote, copied, cared for, and stored their early sacred writings, our understanding of a dark age of history is being greatly expanded. Both Christianity and Judaism will benefit from new manuscripts of the Bible.

4

Muhammed's Legacy

Islam grew from divine revelations to Muhammed and out of the religious concepts of Judaism and Christianity. It was a new faith and it meant a new start for its followers. The new era and calendar date from the Christian year A.D. 622. The believers started a permanent struggle to convert all humanity to Islam; this is the meaning of the term *jihad,* or holy war.

Within the next eighty years the followers of the new faith overran the Arabian peninsula, the Sassanid Empire of Persia, the lands of Palestine, Jordan, and Syria, and the coastal lands of North Africa along the Mediterranean Sea. Within a century, Muslim armies had spread so far east that they were storming the mountain passes of India and had gained access to Spain in the west.

Without deprecating their military achievements, it is only fair to explain that the areas conquered offered little or no resistance to organized assault. The early opponents of Islam were largely unorganized pagan tribes. The Muslims knew whereof they spoke, and the new religion made sense to tribal people. Tribes that were Christians and Jews were not molested because Muhammed considered them fellow "brethren of the book." In the Koran it is expressed: "If your God had pleased, all people on earth would have become Believers. Do you therefore forcibly compel men to become true Believers?" As members of the Islamic community, Jews and Christians were exempt from military service but they did have to pay a special head tax.

Mecca had been a city of holy pilgrimage for the desert dwellers of Arabia from the beginnings of history. A simple building housed a meteoritic stone, rare in that sandy waste, and a collection of 360 carved idols. Muhammed's revolt abolished the idols and substituted a new set of beliefs. The guardians of the sacred stone had been temporal as well as religious leaders. Muhammed became the same, showing outstanding qualities in both theology and political administration.

Muslims believe that God's will and way have been explained by a number of prophets, including Abraham, Moses, and Jesus. Muhammed continues the revelations and is the last person through whom God has spoken. The revelations are recorded in the Koran, a book of 114 chapters, or *suras*. Another book, the Hadith, lists other sayings of Muhammed that were remembered by his companions and associates, recollected by acquaintances and children. Muhammed reviewed the tribal laws and either accepted or revised or rejected them, compiling a source of spiritual law called the *Sunna*. By the second century in the Muslim calender, a group of learned specialists, called *ulema,* had sprung up in different parts of the Islamic world to interpret and expound the intricacies of the law.

Submission to the will of God, or Allah, is the meaning of Islam. Islam requires belief in the Koran and in God. God's angels and apostles must also be believed, because they remind people to be faithful and not superstitious or idol-worshipping. Muslims also believe in a day of judgment and an after-life. As the Koran expresses it: "When a man dies they who survive him ask what property he has left behind. The angel who bends over the dying man asks what good deeds he has sent before him."

Muhammed was an orphan, born about A.D. 570 into a tribe in Arabia that worshipped idols. He grew up to achieve wealth through business and marriage. His life was successful but the people with whom he lived were ignorant, quarrelsome, and superstitious. When he was about forty years old, he claimed that God spoke to him, and Muhammed tried to explain God's revelations to the people in his town of Mecca. People were astonished by his statements that "There is only one God," and angry when he attacked their idols. His statement that "Men are equal, and slaves are not inferior to their masters" was incredible to other tribesmen. As Muhammed preached he gained a few followers, but most of the people were infuriated. Muhammed and his small band were finally driven out of Mecca, going to Medina where they were welcomed.

Muhammed had been persecuted and ridiculed in Mecca, but in leaving he was abandoning the old traditions forever and trusting in the new ways of living that God had outlined. From Medina, Islam spread to many parts of the world. When Muhammed died there was an attempt to deify him, but his successor said: "If there are any among you who worshipped Muhammed, he is dead. But if it was God you worshipped, he lives forever." Muhammed was only the agent for change in God's world.

There are five practices which a faithful Muslim must observe. The first command is to recite the belief in one God, Allah, and in Muhammed as his Prophet. The second devotion is prayer, five times a day in purity; that is, after washing carefully before kneeling and facing toward Mecca. In cities and towns Muslims are reminded to pray by the call of the muezzin from the minaret or tower of the mosque. The muezzin is a trained singer who chants the call to prayer at dawn, noon, midafternoon, sunset, and dusk. Some of the city mosques have been modernized and play a recording through loudspeakers. The muezzin is also caretaker of the mosque.

Friday noon is the time for prayers at the mosque. Here the *Imam,* or prayer leader, will lead the worshippers in passages from the Koran, give a short sermon, and make announcements important to the congregation. Friday is not a holy day of rest as the Christian Sunday used to be, but shops are usually closed during the hour of the service and more and more business firms are closing for the day. That is the only day of the week when Jordanian government offices are closed. It is also a big market day for country people to come to the town to sell their wares or produce.

The mosque may be a simple building of whitewashed mud brick, a converted Byzantine church, or a colorfully tiled jewel of Islamic architecture. A dome identifies a mosque, with one or more minarets beside it. A courtyard provides a pool or basin for the ritual washing. The mosque is a meeting hall for group prayer. Inside the mosque, the floor is covered with carpets and all who enter remove their shoes. In one wall a niche, called a *mihrab,* indicates the direction of Mecca so that even the blind may know the direction in which to pray. There is a pulpit, called a *minbar,* on top of a flight of steps. Sometimes this is made of beautifully carved or inlaid woods. From here the Imam leads the reading of the Koran and preaches on Fridays.

Almsgiving is another practice basic to Islam. Everyone is expected to share with his less fortunate neighbors, either with food or money. If possible the almsgiving should be done personally and humbly, not through some impersonal agency such as the Red Cross or the United Givers. Bequests left for various pious purposes are administered by the *waqf.* These religious groups, directed by *qadis,* or judges, administer the foundations in their districts. The qadis are the local judges of personal and family

The *minbar* stands by a minaret in the Dome of the Rock enclosure.

matters, too, which make them particularly aware of the needs of the community.

The fourth practice is fasting, to remind one of the meager life of the poor. *Ramadan,* the ninth month of the Muslim year, is the month of fasting. Because Muslims use the lunar calendar, the Fast of Ramadan moves progressively eleven days earlier each solar year. When the Fast occurs in the summer months, it becomes an ordeal much more severe than the Christian Lent or the Jewish Passover. It is a real test of self-mastery.

A religious committee in each Muslim country decides when it can first see the new moon in the ninth month. The word is then telegraphed to all the cities. In the villages cannons boom and drums are beaten. Each day thereafter, when at dawn a white thread can first be distinguished from a black one, the Fast begins. The pious Muslim does not eat, drink, or smoke until the guns sound at sunset. Many Muslims wait with a bowl of the "Soup of Ramadan" in their hands, eagerly listening for the first boom. With the end of the long day the family feasts and drinks its fill and then may take a walk in the brief twilight.

Some wealthy families can feast all night and sleep through the day, but the workmen must get some sleep during the all too short night. By one thirty in the morning the quiet of the neighborhood is shattered by a man beating a bass drum, clashing cymbals, and singing at the top of his lungs. He is reminding the families to rise and eat before the early dawn, a custom surviving from the days before alarm clocks.

Muhammed exempted a few persons from the rigor of the Fast: young children, pregnant women, the old, the ill, warriors in battle, and travelers. Some take advantage of these rules, others obey strictly. The end of the month is a three-day celebration, *Id-el-Fitr,* which, when Ramadan occurs during the summer, can be a reward for endurance. Many collapse from heat prostration and dehydration. In order to avoid extreme hardships, the Jordanian government has set short working hours during Ramadan: 9:30 A.M. to 1:30 P.M.

The Id-el-Fitr is a time for exchanging presents and wearing new clothes, feasting, and making calls on friends. The men go to special services at the mosques and the women to the cemeteries, to catch up on the gossip as well as to honor the dead. Schools and businesses close so that everyone can join in the rejoicing. Through it all, drums are beaten, radios are blaring, and in the villages the men dance the native *debke* until exhausted.

This feast is the first three days of the month after Ramadan, the month of *Shawwal*. Jordan also recognizes four other religious holidays: *Muharram* 1, the Muslim New Year's Day; *Rabi al-Awwal* 12, the commemoration of the birth of Muhammed; *Rajab* 27, the feast of *al-Miraj,* celebrating Muhammed's ascension to heaven; and *Dhul-Hijjah* 10, the feast of *al-Adha,* when Muslims who are able make the pilgrimage to Mecca.

The pilgrimage, or *el-Hajj,* is the final discipline. Every Muslim is expected to make the pilgrimage to Mecca at least once during his lifetime. This was not too difficult when Muhammed's followers lived close by, but as Islam spread from Spain to the Philippines, pilgrimages became a vast and complicated business. The hundreds of thousands of pilgrims have to be transported to Mecca at just the right time, housed, fed, clothed in ceremonial garments, and each provided with a ceremonial sheep. The numbers often exceed the tourist facilities or the transportation arrangements of travel agencies.

Pilgrims must plan so that they all arrive at the hostels outside Mecca before the sixth day of Dhul-Hijjah. Weeks before the big event, the ports of the Muslim world are crowded with pilgrims camping on the beaches or on any open space, waiting for the specially chartered pilgrim ships to arrive. It is a once-in-a-lifetime experience for the pilgrim, and aside from the religious meaning of the occasion, it represents a huge investment of time and money.

Pilgrims are met and housed just outside Mecca. They are not allowed to stay unless they have a return ticket home. They bathe and put on special clothing, for men two cotton towels and for women an enveloping black robe and head veil. Exhausting days of ritual follow: circling around the *Kaaba,* the building which originally held the idols destroyed by Muhammed; running between two small hills in the vicinity; offering sacrifices of sheep and camels after a trip to the hill of Arafat twelve miles east of Mecca. Other traditional activities have developed over the years, complicated by increasing numbers of pilgrims crowding the scene.

The final day, the tenth of Dhul-Hijjah, is celebrated throughout the Muslim world. A sheep is sacrificed for a feast; one-third is eaten by a family, one-third is given to relatives, and the last third goes to the poor. During the days that follow, the pilgrims return home. Families are notified of their arrival time. Together with their friends they decorate the house of the pilgrim with palm leaf arches, carpets, or colored lights. Then they hire a taxi and go to the edge of the town or to the airport or dock to greet the traveler. The *hajji,* whether man or woman, is welcomed home with feasting and thanksgiving.

Sometimes a village may have had a resident so holy that after his death the person was declared a saint. This is not orthodox Islam, but is frequent in practice because of the difficulty of a pilgrimage to Mecca. The saint's tomb is the local spot for pilgrimage, where at least once a year religious services are held and prayers are said. There is also frequent reference in conversation to *afrits* and *jinns,* evil spirits which predate Islam. They are lesser forms of paganism, like the malevolent force of the "evil eye," which persist in spite of Islam.

Naturally differences of opinion developed as Islam spread into diverse and distant places. One argument was about the caliphs. At the end of his life, Muhammed dealt more and more with administrative problems, but he did not designate a successor. When Muhammed died in 632 his father-in-law was chosen caliph, following the tribal tradition of selecting the most competent leader available. He died two years later and was succeeded by Omar, the leader of the *jihad.* Ali, Muhammed's adopted son, also wanted to be caliph, and some people supported him. He was brave, but he lacked the necessary qualities of leadership and was killed early in the argument. Ali's supporters went to Persia and established the *Shi'ites,* blending the teachings of Zoroaster with those of Muhammed. The larger orthodox group are called *Sunni.*

In A.D. 661 the center of administration under Caliph Mu'awiyah was moved from Mecca to Damascus, as being more centrally located in their conquered lands. On his deathbed he broke with tribal tradition and designated his son, Zazid I, as successor. Thus was founded the famous Omayyad dynasty that ruled much of the Mediterranean world, including Spain, and for a short time thereafter southern France.

The Omayyads gradually gave up their austere desert habits and enjoyed the soft living and the luxuries of palace life. Unused to administration on a scale larger than a tribe, they hired educated Christians to handle the business details and keep the treasury accounts. Members of the three faiths, Islamic, Jewish, and Christian, lived together quite amicably under one God, whether addressed as Allah, Jehovah, or God.

The Muslim court did not completely forget its desert heritage. Love of hunting, horse racing, and hawking prompted the caliphs to build elaborate hunting lodges in the desert. The lodges, more like small palaces, gave the courtiers an opportunity for freedom from city life and a place to raise and toughen young princes. Jordan has a dozen or more of such desert lodges, of which *Qasr al Amra,* located fifty miles east of Amman, is the best preserved. The triple barrel-vaulted structure sits in a small wadi among green groves of pistachio trees. Beside the big building is a wing of smaller domed structures. Entering a triangular-shaped walled courtyard with cisterns, a doorway leads into the large vaulted audience room with three smaller ones at the far end.

The lower wing of rooms opening off the east side contains the five units of the conventional steam baths.

Most remarkable is the sight of walls and ceilings covered with frescoes, evidently done by foreign artists. Instead of the usual arabesque patterns there are portraits of Arab enemies; scenes of potters at work, carpenters sawing logs, farmers digging, and naturalistic borders of vines. The domed ceiling of the *caldarium,* or hot room, attempts to show the night sky with the constellations. The artists were inaccurate and one wonders how the princes, who knew astronomy well, liked their "planetarium."

Another desert castle, *Qasr al Kharanah,* was built like a fortress. It is a square walled structure with towers at each corner and a single entrance. The stables are on either side as one enters, and the two stories of rooms surround a central courtyard. The most palatial lodge was built by Caliph Hisham Ibn Abdul Malik

Kharanah was built as a desert fortress along the caravan routes.

Hisham's palace near Jericho contained many fine mosaics showing living things, and much intricate plasterwork.

(A.D. 724–743) just north of Jericho and called *Khirbat al Mafjar*. It is a lavish complex of colonnaded courts, baths, and a mosque, with a walled hunting preserve attached to it. In the forecourt was a pool with a domed portico over it and a fountain in the center. The main rooms surrounded a central court richly decorated with carved stucco. The baths had beautiful mosaic floors for the pools and marble-floored hot and cold rooms. Some rooms were heated from a furnace by brick conduits under the floors and around the walls through clay pipes. A water tank for the steam room was built over the furnace. The mosque was square and open to the sky, which was the way mosques were first built, except for a half dome over the wall with the mihrab. The frescoes, the statues, the painted carvings and the plasterwork all give clues to a carefree life of singing and dancing, hunting and bathing, in their vacation houses and before the days when Islamic art excluded human and animal forms.

After A.D. 750 a new dynasty, the Abbasids, moved the capital of the Muslim world to Baghdad. Their conquests moved farther and farther eastward into India and central Asia. Hunting on the desert gave way to the softer influences of the east. Music, poetry, and painting became the court pastimes. Baghdad became the dazzling city of song and story. Harun-al-Rashid (A.D. 786–809) was ruling the vast reaches of Asia and North Africa at the same time that Charlemagne was trying, unsuccessfully, to unite Europe into a Holy Roman Empire.

It was inevitable that such a vast empire, composed of a variety of ethnic groups, would eventually break up. Governors appointed to rule the provinces, such as the territory around Jerusalem, far from central authority, set themselves up as rulers of independent kingdoms and principalities. They paid little or no homage to the Grand Caliph. Only the tenets of the Koran, the sonorous Arabic language, and fusion of the two in prayers at the mosques, kept a tenuous unity for Islam. There were also the pilgrimages to Mecca and Jerusalem.

5

Kerak, Durable Fortress

By the end of the eleventh Christian century a new people, the Turks from beyond the Caspian Sea, had moved westward into Asia Minor. Somewhere along the way they had accepted Islam, but they were not strong enough to consolidate the petty states of the Near East. They did defeat the Byzantine armies sent against them and soon they were threatening the walls of Constantinople itself.

The situation appeared so desperate that the Byzantine emperor, Alexius, appealed to Pope Urban in Rome for help to drive back this horde of infidels. The pope called a council of nobles at Clermont, France, in 1095, and his eloquent appeal launched the First Crusade. Its main object was to take Jerusalem away from its Muslim rulers and "restore it to Christendom."

Seldom had a military expedition set out with more enthusiasm and less sense than the First Crusade. The first wave, under the leadership of Peter the Hermit and Walter the Penniless, was a ragtag mob of human locusts who ate their way across Europe to Constantinople. Alexius hastily ferried them across the Bosporus and the Ottoman Turks massacred them on the plains of Anatolia. The hill of bones left there was a grim warning to subsequent invaders.

The next army consisted largely of Norman princes and their feudal followers. They fared better, being better organized, but it was still a feudal army, units of which were controlled by the whims of their feudal allegiances. Selfish bickering was common among the leaders. The more powerful lords withdrew to carve out kingdoms for themselves along the way at Edessa, Antioch, and Tripoli.

The main body of knights finally reached Jerusalem, thanks more to the disunity of their opponents than to their own military prowess. After naively trying Joshua's tactic, marching

The Crusader castle at Shobak commands a hill between Kerak and Aqaba.

around the city walls blowing trumpets, to no avail, they settled down to the laborious task of a siege. Assault towers were built, tunnels were dug to undermine the walls, and finally, on July 15, 1099, Jerusalem was captured. The Christian victors then indiscriminately massacred some thirty-five thousand men, women, and children until, as one chronicler reported: "In the temple and porch of Solomon men rode in blood up to their knees and bridle reins."

Then Palestine and Jordan were parceled out among land-hungry knights. By Norman policy, strong castles were built to dominate the local inhabitants. The castle of Kerak was such a one, with the added importance that it also controlled the caravan route from Egypt to Syria. The village of Kerak was on the old King's Highway and had been the chief city of Moab.

In Bible times, Kerak was called Kir of Moab and was a bone of contention between the warring peoples during the millennia before Christ. The Romans evidently fortified it as a link in their chain of frontier garrison posts. The Crusader construction, like a huge ship on a towering wave, was a massive fortress on a promontory jutting out of a high plateau. The castle still raises its proud towers three thousand feet above the Dead Sea, and its walls still stand to protect and enclose the modern town.

On one side the Wadi Kerak forms a protective canyon and provides a route that plunges down to the sea thirty miles away. From the castle above, on a clear day, one can recognize not only the southern end of the Dead Sea but also the Mount of Olives at Jerusalem to the north. Across the sea are the pinkish hills of Judea. The slopes fall away on both sides. In Crusader times it was the custom to toss captive enemies off the walls, first thoughtfully enclosing their heads in wooden boxes so they would not be knocked unconscious before crashing on the rocks hundreds of feet below.

The castle was probably built in 1136 by Payem, an Italian nobleman who started out as a cupbearer to King Baldwin II of Jerusalem. His rise to be master of a huge and important castle was typical of the opportunities open to ambitious young men determined to make their fortunes in the East. It is fitting that now a hospital-hospice, maintained by an Italian order of nursing nuns, has been built on the foundations of the inner keep of the castle of Kerak.

Huge storehouses lie under the main level of the courtyards. The latter are lined with galleries, the walls of which are loopholed for archers. At the extreme tip of the high spur, before it falls away to the wadis on either side, the noble apartments of the ruling family still stand intact and can easily be imagined populated with lord, wife and children, squires, pages, secretaries, servants, and at least one learned Arab doctor.

When Saladin, leader of the Muslim forces, first attacked the castle in 1173 it was defended by the wife of the owner. Stephanie of Milly filled her water tanks, brought her serfs, cattle, and grain within the walls, blocked the two tunnel entrances to the castle, and when night came, signaled by bonfire to Jerusalem for help. The threat of reinforcements from Jerusalem caused Saladin to withdraw to Egypt.

The next year King Amalric of Jerusalem died, leaving the kingdom to his thirteen-year-old son Baldwin IV. He had been attending a school for future knights where one of the juvenile tests of courage was to stick pins into each other's arms. Baldwin showed the most bravery by his unflinching resistance to pain. Then it was discovered that his insensitivity was due to leprosy.

Miles of Plancy, Stephanie's husband, was named regent. He was assassinated shortly afterward and Stephanie married an unscrupulous adventurer named Reynald of Chatillon. In the meantime, the boy king's leprosy had grown rapidly worse. Realizing

The castle at Kerak dominates the present-day town as well as the Dead Sea valley.

his desperate situation, King Baldwin made a truce with Saladin which guaranteed safe movement of Christian and Muslim merchant caravans through each other's territory.

Unfortunately Reynald, now Lord of Kerak, who would be characterized today as a ruthless operator, could not resist capturing a rich caravan on its way to Mecca in July, 1181. Such treachery was unforgivable by Arab standards. Saladin declared war and campaigned in the northern area of the Kingdom of Jerusalem. Reynald persisted in his wicked ways even to equipping a pirate fleet at Aqaba to prey on the African coast. Saladin was naturally incensed at this new breach of faith, and sent his armies into Jordan.

The little daughter of King Amalric had become engaged to Stephanie's son Humphrey, meanwhile, and in spite of threats of war Stephanie was determined to make the wedding the grandest in the history of Jordan. Christian nobles from as far north as Antioch were invited to the nuptials. In the midst of the festivities, Saladin and his army arrived to besiege Kerak.

Lady Stephanie sent banquet dishes to Saladin and he in turn politely asked where the newly wed couple would be housed so that he could avoid bombarding that section of the castle. A bonfire message to Jerusalem brought reinforcements and for the second time Saladin withdrew his troops. In 1186 Reynald captured another rich caravan and refused to talk to an envoy from Saladin.

The Muslim governors were summoned to avenge the treachery. A Frankish army under the leadership of weak Guy of Lusingnan, successor to Baldwin IV, made a forced march to the Horns of Hattin, two rocky hills north of Tiberias on the west side of the Jordan River. The well there was found to be dry and the exhausted men spent a miserable night. Their misery was aggravated by the Muslims firing dry grass which sent choking clouds of smoke over the Crusader camp. The battle began at dawn, July 4, 1187, and by midafternoon only a handful of knights, including King Guy and Reynald, were left, too tired to raise their weapons.

The king and nobles were sent to Damascus as prisoners but Saladin himself cut off the head of treacherous Reynald of Kerak. The castle was captured but Stephanie was courteously allowed to go to Tripoli, the stronghold of Count Raymond. Soon Tiberias and Nablus fell to the victorious Muslims. On Friday, October 2, 1187, the anniversary of the day when Muhammed had visited the city before ascending to heaven, Saladin entered Jerusalem.

Two years later Saladin took the only other important Crusader castle east of the Jordan River. Located at Shobak, halfway between Kerak and Aqaba, it stands on an isolated hill. King Baldwin I of Jerusalem built it in 1115 to control further the caravan route between Egypt and Damascus.

In less than two centuries the ill-started attempt to turn the Near East into a Christian domain had failed. When the first army of Crusaders arrived in the Holy Land, they did not realize that they had come when the area was torn with squabbles among their Arab and Seljuk Turk enemies. As a consequence the Christian nobles were able to carve out feudal states for themselves with comparative ease. Although the Kingdom of Jerusalem sounded impressive to European ears, it was ever the victim of petty intrigue, vain ambition, and the downright treachery of its rulers.

After the capture of Jerusalem by the consolidated Muslim armies, the Crusaders were slowly pushed to a fringe of coastal castles, such as Tyre, Sidon, Byblos, and Tripoli, that could be supplied and garrisoned by Western ships. Venice and Genoa grew wealthy on this futile shuttling of supplies and men. Waves of religious enthusiasm ebbed and flowed across Europe, but each wave was smaller and the results less effective in sustaining the Crusader effort.

The first generation of Crusaders, willing to settle down amiably among their Arab neighbors, appreciated the superior culture of the Arabs in science, mathematics, medicine, astronomy, and military architecture. The Arabs taught them a great deal about diseases and their treatment, surgical instruments, and chemical substances. Scientific methods of observation and experiment, as well as the knowledge acquired, were to influence European scientists for several centuries. Many of the distinctive features of castles, the crenellated walls, the battlements and towers boldly protruding from the walls to provide flanking fire along the walls, were developed by the Arabs and taken back to France and England by the Crusaders.

The Crusader women quickly learned to like such fabrics as silk, taffeta, muslin, brocades, and cottons. Oriental perfumes added to their charm and exquisite jewelry of gold and precious stones to their pride. Their lot was softened through the influence of Arab respect for and protection of their women. Arab poetry and songs of romance became their entertainment. They even learned about bathing!

Probably the greatest contribution was in the realm of food. The rather limited diet of Europe was enriched by the discovery of sugarcane and fruits: oranges, lemons, pomegranates, strawberries, apricots, bananas, and peaches. Muslim traders introduced rice and buckwheat from China, a variety of delicious melons from Persia, and spices from India. Spices made it possible to treat the barrels of salted meat, beginning to spoil after a long winter, in a way to make it edible. Mincemeat was a product of necessity and spices.

The Crusaders also learned that the "infidel" had a social and religious tolerance that was rare in Europe at that time. Scholarship and culture, with the barriers broken and new routes of exchange open, spread to Europe. When the last Crusaders were driven from the Island of Arwad, off the coast of Syria, to take refuge on the Island of Cyprus in 1302, the Holy Land was left to the Muslims for whom it was equally holy.

6

Two Banks of a River

For nearly five centuries the Arab people were part of the Ottoman Empire. Turkish authority was often weak but it was always there as a positive check on Arab nationalism and independence. Local communities were seldom disturbed and custom and traditional law prevailed. Religious communities were left to govern themselves and only through taxes did the people feel the restrictions of Turkish rule. Nothing much was done for them but nothing much was done to restrict them, except in the case of local corrupt officials.

In 1900 Sultan Abdul Hamid proposed to Turkey that all Muslim countries help to build a railroad from Damascus to Medina for the comfort of pilgrims on their way to Mecca. The idea caught on and the railroad was completed by 1908. Only Sherif Hussein, head of the Hashemite family, a direct descendant of Muhammed and guardian of the sacred city of Mecca, doubted the sultan's pious concern for the pilgrims. Sherif Hussein suspected, and rightly, that the wily sultan was more interested in using the railroad to move troops into the Arabian peninsula called the Hejaz. The tribes of Arabia had only their religion in common with the Ottoman Turks and had been left pretty much alone. Now the picture was changing.

Sherif Hussein had spent fifteen years in Constantinople at the request of the sultan, and his four sons had been educated there. Hussein knew about the Turks firsthand. Early in 1914 he asked the British government to help the Arabs gain independence from the Turks. At first Britain was not interested but Britain's emmissary in Cairo for a second meeting, Henry McMahon, agreed: "Great Britain is prepared to recognize and support the independence of the Arabs in all regions within the limits demanded by the Sherif of Mecca."

By this time, October, 1915, Turkey had sided with Germany in World War I. The Arabs revolted from Ottoman rule led by Hussein and his four sons, Ali, Abdullah, Feisal, and Said, and supplied with guns by British agents. T. E. Lawrence, or Lawrence of Arabia, one of these agents, caught the public eye with his dashing hit-and-run raids on the "pilgrim railroad," but he was only one of many dedicated British advisers. By ripping up rails and blowing up culverts and bridges, the raiders succeeded in isolating large numbers of Turkish troops in their garrisons. As the Arabs advanced northward, more and more fighting men joined their cause. Meanwhile the British army was fighting in a parallel line to the west; the two armies met in Damascus on October 2, 1918. The Turks were defeated and the Ottoman Empire came to an end.

In 1916, without acknowledging the McMahon-Hussein correspondence, Britain and France approved in secret the Sykes-Picot Agreement which cut the Middle East into spheres of influence. It proposed that Jerusalem and its environs be made an international area. Palestine was to remain a separate entity under Britain, and France claimed Lebanon and northern Syria because of the desires of a small Christian minority.

The next year the promise for independence to the Arabs was double-crossed in another way. The British Secretary of State for

Foreign Affairs, Arthur Balfour, wrote a letter to Lord Rothschild which said: "His Majesty's Government view with favour the establishment in Palestine of a national home for the Jewish people, and will use their best endeavours to facilitate achievement of this object, it being clearly understood that nothing shall be done which may prejudice the civil and religious rights of existing non-Jewish communities in Palestine. . . ."

Lord Rothschild was a wealthy Jew who had supported colonies of Jewish immigrants to Palestine. He was not a member of the World Zionist Organization which was trying to find a place where Jews could live separately without discrimination or persecution, but he shared the letter with his coreligionists. The Zionists had asked Britain for support before and had been offered land in Africa. They had decided, after discussing the matter with Jews living in many countries, that they wanted to live in Palestine which was the site of their Biblical history. From the moment the Zionists received Lord Balfour's message, they were relentless in pursuing their idea of a "national home." It also meant that Jews intended to be a national group as well as a religious faith.

The fact that Britain had made two other agreements directly opposed to theirs did not matter to the Zionists nor for some time did it matter greatly to Britain. The Arabs were not concerned by other promises because they knew they had earned their independence and the right to decide their future. Hussein's son Feisal received a tumultuous welcome when he got to Damascus and was crowned king at an Arab Congress meeting in March, 1920. He was, so the Arabs said, to rule all of Syria including Lebanon, Transjordan, and Palestine. The world powers, however, preferred to cut up the territory between France and Britain who would administer mandates from the League of Nations. President Wilson sent the King-Crane Commission to Palestine and

Syria to interview the population; the inhabitants repeated their claim and desire to rule themselves. The final answer for the Arabs was for France to administer the northern area, split into Lebanon and Syria, and for Britain to administer Palestine. Hussein's help during the war was honored to the extent that, since his son Feisal could not be king of Damascus, Feisal was made king of Iraq under special British sponsorship.

The boundaries of the new territories were arbitrarily drawn by Britain and France, more concerned with the spoils of war than with the nationalist interests of the people concerned. There had been no opportunity for local government to develop, for national leaders to emerge. Foreign troops remained on Middle Eastern soil and vested interests were often encouraged by the mandate authorities. The Arabs became more isolated from one another than encouraged towards self-government. The Jordan River became the line dividing Palestine on the west and Transjordan on the east bank.

TRANSJORDAN

Emir Abdullah, another of Hussein's sons, quietly recruited a private army of two hundred and appeared in Ma'an in January of 1921. He vowed to continue north and drive the French out of Syria. Lacking any policy directives from either Great Britain or the League of Nations, the British agents in Kerak arranged for Abdullah to set up a government at Amman. The Emirate of Transjordan was set up in March of the same year.

On May 26, 1923, Great Britain recognized Transjordan as an autonomous state under the League mandate. Great Britain provided a financial subsidy and reserved the right to control foreign policy and supervise finances. Abdullah was not daunted by organizing a new country under these limitations and, despite criticism from the Arabs, never forsook his loyalty to Britain. Emir

Abdullah enlisted some experienced Arab administrators from Damascus. Many more flocked around him who turned out to be malcontents and plotters. He made a point to visit and become acquainted with the tribes and was always available to personal appeals for justice or to redress wrongs. He wisely based his organization on expanded tribal law and custom.

A police force was needed to safeguard the authority of the central government in Amman. The most pressing problem was to stop tribal warfare and raiding across the borders. The Bedouin tribes had long raided each other and the custom, centuries old, was hard to suppress. Such a force was organized, based on Abdullah's original two hundred supporters. Abdullah asked Captain F. G. Peake of the Egyptian Camel Corps to build up a desert patrol for Transjordan. Peake and his corps had fought beside the Arab army from Aqaba to Damascus in World War I, so he was not a stranger to the country and its people. He was a strikingly tall man, nicknamed "Thunder Cloud" by his troops. He achieved remarkable results by appearing to be always angry about everything and with everybody.

Peake assigned one hundred men to a Mobile Force to guard the Amman-Palestine Road. Fifty men were stationed in Kerak to help the British representative. Syrians and Palestinians from the Turkish army were enlisted because the Bedouins were suspicious of the new central government and its army. In 1923 the security forces were reorganized as the Arab Legion, and Peake was made commander and designated brigadier general.

A Frontier Force was established in 1926 to guard the long and often desolate border. Composed of British troops, it was not a satisfactory solution to the border problems particularly in the south. For 150 miles that border consisted of the east-west range of the Tubeiq Mountains. They formed a spectacular wall, rising abruptly out of the desert, but contained numerous canyons for the convenience of raiding parties.

It was time for Transjordan to expand the Arab Legion to include a Desert Mobile Force. John Bagot Glubb, an experienced British officer from Iraq, was asked in 1930 to take the job and organize such a force. He was an ideal choice; he spoke Arabic fluently, was infinitely patient, understood and admired the desert Arabs. He made a good second-in-command to Peake.

With infinite patience and tact, Glubb slowly won recruits from the important desert tribes. Eventually, by careful selection of recruits and intensive training, the Desert Mobile Force became the striking element of the Jordan army. The names of eager volunteers were on a long list awaiting openings for enlistments. The Legion recruits were not only trained in the use of arms and modern transport but also taught to read and write. More important, there gradually grew up an *esprit de corps,* a high morale and loyalty that made the Legion a unique body of proud men dedicated to their task of patrolling 750 miles of Jordanian borders.

A treaty signed in 1932 between the heads of Jordan and Saudi Arabia formally stopped raids on the southern border. But the northern border was still a tough problem. At its western end the border ran through one hundred miles of black lava boulders. On the plains farther east the Syrian tribes were accustomed to winter-graze in Jordan. The French, who held Syria under the Mandate, were usually indifferent to the problems of tribal raids and uncooperative about curbing smuggling.

The desert of boulders was the hideout of small tribes called collectively "the people of the mountain." They were a mean people, dressed in rags and dirty sheepskin coats. Goats and a few sheep provided a sparse existence. For extras they would creep out at night, raid a village or a Bedouin camp, and be back to their inaccessible hideout by daybreak. Prying a path through the boulders, the Legion slowly cut roads through the area wide enough for armored trucks. After a few quick reprisal raids the mountain tribes mended their ways. For the rest of the north border a joint commission was set up to settle disputes and assess damages.

Emir Abdullah had worked wisely and well to bring together the diverse groups within his territory. Slowly the Bedouins agreed to accept Abdullah's leadership, surrendering their traditional authority, and to join the Arab Legion. Abdullah was fortunate in a royal heritage that made him instinctively the charming host and the courteous diplomat. He and George VI of Great Britain shared interests in hunting and horses as well as in governing. When in 1936 he entertained Prince Saud Ibn Saud of Saudi Arabia, his gracious hospitality ignored the fact that the two royal houses had been enemies for generations.

The British, under the Mandate, gradually separated the administration of Transjordan from the overrule of the British High Commissioner in Jerusalem. A British Resident in Amman became political adviser to Abdullah. His duties were to oversee foreign affairs, the budget (because Transjordan was economically insufficient), mineral resources, and foreigners in the area. Foreigners were more clearly defined by a Law of Nationality in 1928 which defined nationals as anyone who had been living in Transjordan in 1924. This limited the activities of educated, urban Arab nationalists from Egypt, Syria, and Palestine who opposed Abdullah and also gave the less educated residents a better chance for jobs in the government.

Also in 1928 the Organic Law was passed, outlining government responsibilities and limits. A Legislative Council was established to develop law, which the emir would pass or veto. The emir still had the authority to rule by decree, and the British Resident to overrule the entire decision. An Electoral Law was passed the same year. These laws were expanded in 1941 when the British gave Transjordan more autonomy and Abdullah set up a cabinet arranged by departments.

There were revolts, there were riots, there were intrigues against Abdullah and his dream for a free country. To those who knew him well, Abdullah was a kindly man, sometimes difficult but fair and farsighted in his decisions. The king loved all the trappings of royalty, the ceremony and pomp, but retained the unusual ability to laugh at himself as well as to enjoy a good joke on others. Always a realist, he proposed moderation and compromise. In 1934 he proposed, and was supported by a British Royal Commission, that if Palestine were partitioned the Arab state in Palestine be merged with Transjordan.

In 1939 Glubb took over from Peake as commander of the Arab Legion as if anticipating a shift in emphasis to fighting on the fringes of World War II. The Arab Legion continued to build roads and was often called upon to help villagers dig wells or to provide medical care. In the larger sense, it was a supportive job the Legion did in the next few years. Britain and Abdullah conferred and it was decided to double Transjordan's force with Britain supplying the arms and mechanized vehicles. When supply lines were cut, Jordan had to improvise equipment.

The Germans, after they had defeated France itself, took over its mandates in Syria and Lebanon and encouraged a *coup d'etat* in Iraq. The Iraqi Hashemites went into exile in Jerusalem. In fighting between the Iraqi army and the British the Arab Legion was dispatched to help the British, and eventually the British-sponsored Hashemite government was restored to power. The Arab Legion also helped the British army on the Syrian front and in Sinai when German General Rommel's forces were threatening

Egypt. The Arab Legion guarded supply lines, supply dumps, bridges, railway lines, airports, and pipelines. It was an unglamorous job but the Legion performed it faithfully and well.

PALESTINE

In Palestine Britain was trying to sort out its promises. There was much more Arab resistance to creating a Jewish home in Palestine than had been foreseen by the British government. Arabs rioted when, in 1918, a Zionist Commission arrived in the country, led by Chaim Weizmann, demanding participation in administration and space for new immigrants. The Arabs were astonished, then suspicious, and finally enraged by the betrayal of the promise of independence. The Arab population was already unified by language and culture; they did not want to be subjugated economically or politically. As they saw more and more Jews entering their country they were apprehensive. They demanded a national government to be chosen by all the people of the country, Muslims, Christians, and Jews.

Britain did not listen, or at least it did not act. Jews continued to pour into the area at an increasing rate. In the 1880's the Jews represented 5 percent of the total population; by the end of World War I, further colonies of settlers had brought the proportion to 10 percent. By 1924 the percentage had risen to 13.4 and by 1940 it had escalated to 31.4 percent. Whenever the Zionists needed support for their activities they appealed to their members in the various countries. Other Jewish viewpoints were not heard any more than the Arabs. As Hitler increased his program to get rid of all the Jews in Germany, Palestine was handed the responsibility for resettling them. It was an imposed solution, not taking into account a long-settled population already living in Palestine and a limited amount of good land.

From the beginning of the Mandate, Britain tried to believe

that its dual promises could be fulfilled. The Arabs never accepted the Mandate because of the false premise on which it was based: that the Palestinians wanted to get along with a Jewish population which was intent upon becoming the majority and deporting the Arabs who had always lived there. The Zionists, and the countries they had gotten to support them, disregarded the fact that more immigrants into Palestine meant more friction, more need for outside money, more industries for which there were no raw materials. The newly arrived Jews did not try to get along with the Arabs, as the original Jews had; they wanted separate schools, farm areas, towns, and businesses. Jews bought land from absentee non-Palestinian landlords and from landholders who did not realize the threat of Zionism.

The Zionists found a well-developed economy when they came to Palestine, with a thriving citrus industry. There were a soap industry and a textile industry and several Arab banks with sizeable accounts. All this had been accomplished without outside help or the capital which Zionists brought with them. The overloaded economy suffered, however, with high prices and two "crashes" that did not occur elsewhere in the Middle East.

The Palestinians rioted in 1920, 1921, 1925, 1929, 1933, and from 1936 until 1939 when World War II began; in fact, every time conditions got ·particularly intolerable. As time went on, guerrilla groups were formed by the Arabs to fight immigration of Jews, and by the Jews to terrorize the Palestinians into cooperation. Arabs were evicted from their land, and in some cases whole villages were wiped out, for which there was no restitution or compensation. In 1939 the British amended their policy statement to say that Palestine should not become part of a Jewish state, but no one paid any attention; world events overtook the situation. Europe went to war, the Arabs helped the Allies in supportive battles in the Middle East, and the Zionists moved their campaign for support to the United States while recruiting young Jews in Europe to go to Palestine to prepare a Jewish army.

A Commission of Inquiry, set up by the British and Americans in 1946, recommended that Palestine be put under the trusteeship of the United Nations. This did not win support from anybody. The Arabs maintained that it continued the Mandate situation whereby the Zionists could rely on Great Britain and America to protect them from the consequences of their refusal to seek Arab friendship. As the Arab League expressed it in their appeal to the United Nations: "It is possible to consider the Palestinian question from two points of view which cannot be reconciled with one another and between which a choice must be made: either (a) the rights, interests and wishes of the existing population are to be regarded as paramount in accordance with normal democratic principles, or (b) it may be considered from the point of view of the world Jewish problem: that is to say, it may be decided that the needs of a people who have never lived in Palestine and who have no real connection with it are more important than the wishes and rights of the existing population which can be ignored or overridden."

After hearing the appeal from the Arab League, hearing statements from the World Zionist Organization, and visiting the area, the Comission of Inquiry recommended the partition of Palestine into a Jewish and an Arab state, with the United Nations overseeing Jerusalem and the holy places. Neither the Arabs nor the Jews accepted the idea. Even if they had wanted to make it work, the plan was unworkable. Each group was given three sections of Palestine, each touching only at a corner, and with the Arabs given Jaffa which was completely surrounded by Israeli territory. There was to be an economic union, said the United Nations, which would have been necessary and inevitable under the plan.

The United Nations General Assembly went ahead and approved partition on November 22, 1947. The United States pressured many countries into voting for the plan, and only the Islamic countries plus Greece and Cuba voted against it. In Palestine fighting broke out in earnest as soon as the UN decision was announced. Troops from Egypt, Syria, and Iraq, operating independently and under no unified command, entered Palestine to support the Arabs. The British tried belatedly to blockade the coast against further ships full of immigrants. Eventually arms, paid for by American Zionists, began to arrive and the Arabs were defeated in a series of battles. On May 14, 1948, Israel proclaimed itself an independent nation. The last of the British Mandate troops left the next day.

The one positive action Britain had taken was to give Transjordan its independence, making Emir Abdullah the king. The Arab Legion was still dependent on the British army, however, for leadership, supplies, and arms. When the British left Palestine they took these services as well as their air cover, medical corps, and trucks. The armies of Egypt, Iraq, Lebanon, and Syria, which joined the Legion in the battle to save Palestine, were less prepared and no better equipped or trained for sudden call-up. Lebanon and Syria were brand-new nations with no trained leadership. The Zionists, on the other hand, had prepared for this moment, were well supplied with arms and equipment, and were fighting in a limited geographical space (as compared to the thousands of miles that many of the other troops had traveled to get there).

After a month of fighting, the Security Council arranged a truce, and then another. The first United Nations mediator, Count Folke Bernadotte of Sweden, was assassinated by Israeli terrorists in Israeli-held territory after only four months of negotiations. No final armistice agreement was reached until the spring of 1949. This was not a peace settlement, although the mediator, Ralph Bunche of the United States, received the Nobel Peace Prize; it was a hasty, unsatisfactory agreement to keep the peace along the lines established as temporary borders. No political settlement has ever been made and the boundary lines are still in dispute.

7

The Hashemite Kingdom of Jordan

On March 22, 1946, Transjordan was granted full independence from the Mandate held by Great Britain. Abdullah was crowned king in May and the new constitution, for a fully independent system of government, was adopted in December.

After his coronation, King Abdullah proposed that Transjordan and Syria merge. In their original negotiations with Britain during World War I, the Arabs had made it clear that they did not want the French to control Syria. In fact, Syria and Palestine were considered one entity by the Arabs; it was the European powers that arbitrarily divided them. The Syrians had their own ideas of national independence and declined. Transjordan was the weaker country and the more vulnerable because of its closeness to Palestine and because it had no natural resources. Abdullah then asked Iraq to consider a union and again his offer was refused.

By this time, in 1948, fighting was heavy in Palestine and the Arab Legion, joined by other Arab forces, was trying to hold onto the areas of Palestine designated for the Arabs in the partition plan. The Arab forces were only partially successful but all the Muslims were particularly thankful that the holy Old City of Jerusalem was saved. When the truce was arranged the Zionists had

King Abdullah stands beneath a portrait of his father, Sherif Hussein.

gained about a third more land than they had been assigned. The
Palestinians were left with two unconnected portions, Gaza on
the Mediterranean Sea and the West Bank of the Jordan River.
Gaza declared itself an independent state in September, 1949, but
in December a congress of religious leaders, tribal chiefs, and del-
egates from refugee camps was held in Jericho, overrode that de-

cision, and voted for union with Transjordan. This action was rat-
ified by the Jordanian Cabinet and Legislature and on April 24,
1950, Transjordan became the Hashemite Kingdom of Jordan.
Gaza was put under UN administration.

Overnight Jordan's population was increased both in numbers
and in range of opinions. The Palestinians were better educated,
more skilled than the Transjordanians, and had a national spirit
of their own. In their heart of hearts they did not accept the king
as their leader. As time went on, the skilled Palestinian refugees
all found jobs in Jordan or in other Arab countries that desperately needed their abilities. But the great majority of the refugees
were unskilled and unemployable anywhere because the whole
Middle East region, in an era of development and industriali-
zation, needed fewer rather than more farmers. The refugees were
willing to work but there was no land to farm; they were willing
to be trained but Jordan had few vocational schools. Nor could
the Jordan national budget afford such a large welfare population. The refugees had to remain in camps not because Jordan
wanted them to remain unsettled but because Jordan had no resources for remaking their lives.

Seven hundred thousand frightened, fleeing people is not an
easy number to handle. Immediately the Arab countries began relief services, assisted by volunteer agencies. Even those refugees
who had money discovered that their funds were frozen in banks
in Israel. Resourceful refugees got jobs or went to countries
where they could be employed or moved in with relatives. In the
course of twenty years many of the original group have ceased to
be refugees, but in the meantime five hundred thousand new refugees have been born and reached maturity.

Sometimes home was a shanty of scraps, corrugated iron, and
rags; sometimes a tent or a mud hut. Any of these could easily

blow down or be flooded by a rainstorm. Who would rebuild these fragile habitations, when the dwellers were old, sick, or cold? Who would help a neighbor if one couldn't help oneself? The dwellings of whatever sort were huddled together, with scant space for each family, along narrow lanes. There were no provisions for human waste or garbage at the beginning. There was no community organization. The old died of exposure and the young of malnutrition, the healthy fought the spread of disease and the ravages of mice and other pests. How does one live, confined by acres and acres of other human beings, disfigured, discouraged, deformed, and harassed, either initially or as time wears on in the refugee camp?

When the United Nations Relief and Works Agency (UNRWA) was mobilized to help with the refugees, it started operations by dispensing food and building temporary dwellings. These often became permanent towns as did the camp near Jericho. Basic food, shelter, and welfare services cost UNRWA an average of five cents a day per person; medical and sanitation, one cent; education and training, four cents; and this adds up to a ten-cent-a-day per refugee expense. UNRWA's vocational training program was initiated by John Davis, an American, when he was Commissioner-General, and it has made the most significant contribution towards solving the long-term needs of the refugees. Over one hundred thousand refugees are presently students in the UNRWA-sponsored schools in Jordan: elementary, secondary, vocational, and teacher training schools. These schools have eased the burden on the national education system. UNRWA cooperates with the World Health Organization and UNESCO and UNICEF for special services. Many voluntary agencies like the International Red Cross and the Lutheran World Federation work with the refugees, too, continuing the jobs they began before UNRWA could step in.

Palestinian refugee women fill their pails at the water point in an UNRWA camp.

Getting the camps organized and the needs of the camp dwellers sorted out did not happen all at once. There was confusion, misunderstanding, and personal tragedy in the lives of many Palestinians. Families were separated, children got lost from their parents, rations were often short for the need. Jordanians often resented refugees swarming into their towns or rural areas, over-taxing limited water and food supplies and the resources for sustaining an increased population.

Political unrest and subversive agitation worsened in 1951. An unusual drought ruined three-fourths of the wheat and barley crop. Food shortages and rising prices added to the general discontent of both Jordanians and Palestinians. Extremists were looking for a scapegoat on whom to blame their troubles. Radio Cairo and Radio Baghdad tried to promote their own interests in Jordan. In 1945 Jordan had joined the Arab League, an association with Iraq, Lebanon, Saudi Arabia, Egypt, Syria, and Yemen. (In 1959 Libya, Morocco, Sudan, and Tunisia, and in 1961 Kuwait, joined the original group.) King Abdullah was not a popular head of state among the members. He was accused of being a stooge of Britain and in league with the Zionists to get the West Bank.

King Abdullah had innate dignity and single-mindedness in working out what was best for Jordan. He was also taking into account Crown Prince Talal's periodic attacks of schizophrenia. Talal was a dubious successor, so the king supervised the education of his grandson Hussein from an early age. King Abdullah took Hussein with him on visits to the desert tribes and taught him the rules of conduct becoming a future monarch, as well as Muslim law and Middle Eastern politics.

On Friday, July 20, 1951, King Abdullah prepared to leave Amman with his grandson to attend religious services at the al-Aqsa mosque in Jerusalem, as was his custom. There was tension in the city and advisers feared an attack might be made on the king. Many of the king's courtiers were reluctant to attend the service with him. Perhaps it was a premonition of tragedy that prompted the king to insist that sixteen-year-old Hussein change into his dress uniform, complete with medals, for the occasion. Arriving at the mosque, King Abdullah rebuked the augmented guard of honor for such noisy ceremony in a holy place. As the king turned to enter the mosque, a man stepped from behind the door and shot him dead. Young Hussein rushed at the assassin, who shot him in the chest before being killed himself by the palace guards.

The young prince reeled as the assassin shot him but by a miracle the bullet glanced off a medal and Hussein escaped unharmed. Stunned by the tragedy, the boy stood petrified until a member of the Royal Air Force, Jock Dalgleish, took him away and flew him to Amman. The crown prince, now King Talal, was in Switzerland for treatment. An interim cabinet ran the country until he could return.

Contrary to popular ideas of royalty, Crown Prince Hussein had been brought up in an atmosphere close to poverty. The Hashemite family had lost their lands and the guardianship of Mecca to King Ibn Saud and his *Wahhabi* tribesmen. The British paid King Abdullah a small subsidy, and with this money Hussein was sent to Victoria College in Alexandria, Egypt, for two years of instruction in Arabic and English. With his grandfather's death it was impossible to return to Egypt. Finally it was arranged that he attend Harrow, one of Britain's exclusive preparatory schools for boys. There he joined his cousin Feisal from Iraq. The adjustment for both boys was rugged; they had to learn to think in English and to adapt themselves to a rigid discipline, strange foods, and new games.

The next year Hussein was vacationing with his mother in Switzerland when a cable announced that King Talal had been deposed as mentally incompetent by an act of the Council of Representatives. The seventeen-year-old boy suddenly became king under the guidance of a regency council. Returning to Amman, he was ceremoniously welcomed by officials and honor guard. In the streets a warm, noisy, friendly crowd welcomed him, too, confirming his determination to do the best he could for his people.

Since the king could not be proclaimed until he reached his

eighteenth birthday, he had idle months to fill. He visited all the desert tribes to get acquainted with their sheiks. That accomplished, he went to Britain for a six months' special course at the Royal Military Academy at Sandhurst. In April, 1953, he returned to Amman and his duties as king. That same year his cousin Feisal became king of Iraq.

There was much rejoicing in Amman when, on April 19, 1955, King Hussein I married Sharifa Dina Abdul-Hamed, a distant cousin. Amman was gaily decorated with flags and banners of welcome, bearing portraits of the king and queen. Unfortunately the marriage proved to be unhappy and was dissolved after eighteen months, during which a daughter Alia was born.

King Hussein learned to fly under the tutelage of the Royal Air Force officer who had flown him back to Amman after his grandfather's murder. He hoped that his learning to fly would inspire some of his subjects to do the same. It was also his hope to build up an efficient, dedicated air force. His flying gave him freedom from tensions and mundane cares, and the exhilaration experienced by all who have piloted planes.

At first the young king was inclined to take his administrative duties rather casually but national events forced Hussein to take decisive action. When Iraq signed the Baghdad Pact in 1955 without consulting the other Arab countries, Egypt in particular was angered. The pact was with Britain and Turkey to form a defensive military wall against Russian aggression. When Jordan was asked to join, rioting broke out in Amman, the cabinet fell, and finally King Hussein dissolved the government. A new government was formed that opposed the pact but the turmoil caused loss of life and an immense amount of damage to government buildings and foreign property.

During the turmoil there was great pressure from Jordanians and Egyptians on King Hussein to fire General Glubb as commanding general of the Arab Legion. The Arab Legion had become the regular army of Jordan, instead of an internal security force, after Transjordan became independent. Glubb was still in command, and Jordanians increasingly resented the British influence he represented. Early in 1956 General Glubb was asked to resign from the Arab Legion he had helped to create, and in the autumn the pro-Egyptian faction, admiring Egypt's control of the Suez Canal and acquisition of arms from the Soviets, was well represented in the elections.

The Arab Legion was renamed the Jordan Army with a Jordanian as its commanding officer. The king remained as the commander-in-chief and had cause the next year to fire his chief-of-staff for plotting with the prime minister to overthrow him. Army training is still augmented by foreigners but basic skills are taught at the Royal Military Academy and, for officers, at the Royal Staff College. The Royal Jordanian Navy is part of the army, since its duties are limited to patrol craft for the Dead Sea and the Gulf of Aqaba. The Royal Jordanian Air Force handles air power, while the army is composed of the infantry and armored brigades.

The police force was separated from the Arab Legion in laws of 1956 and 1958 to form the Public Security Force. It is under the Ministry of the Interior, except in times of war when it is directed from the Ministry of Defense. Its organization, as in most police forces, is military. Its duties include road traffic, firearms and explosives, prisons, communications, criminal investigation, civil defense, and transportation. The Jordan police also provide tourist information, search for missing persons, guard shrines, and render first aid. The Royal Police Academy is the principal training center.

There are ten police districts in the country, eight of them corresponding to the governmental districts of the country. The

Amman district outside the city proper is separate and handles the guarding of airport, railroad station, and palace. The tenth district is the desert patrol to supervise the Bedouin and tribal courts. It is equipped with camels, horses, and four-wheel-drive vehicles.

The emphasis is on crime prevention rather than crime detection, and the suspect is innocent until proved guilty in court by the bulk of evidence. There is a special juvenile court system and a series of detention homes for juveniles, but the majority of juvenile crimes are settled within the family system. Crimes against

The Desert Patrol uses camels as well as four-wheel drive trucks.

property are more common than crimes against persons. Most crimes are punished by imprisonment or fine but sometimes the judge simply gives a reprimand. Temporary or permanent hard labor is the sentence for many serious crimes. Capital punishment, death by hanging, is seldom used except in espionage cases.

The Public Security Directorate coordinates efforts with governors of the provinces and the Ministry of Social Welfare to decrease poverty and increase employment opportunities. It has also adopted more modern and scientific methods of crime prevention and detection in recent years. The Narcotics Office cooperates with similar agencies in other Arab League countries to put down smuggling, peddling, and addiction, and built a new reformatory hospital for addicts. The police force is the staff of the prisons. The area prisons are in the large towns such as Amman and Irbid, and jails are located in the smaller towns. Jordan recognizes rehabilitation rather than retribution as the central focus of imprisonment. Prisons have the usual educational, vocational, and other services but as in other countries Jordan is trying to provide better facilities and trained personnel. The success of the present rehabilitative programs can be measured by the low rate of recidivism, and the system as a whole by the low crime rate.

This may in part be due to a carry-over from the traditions of the Arab Legion, making the police force the paternal advisers to the people in their districts. The police know where the doctor is in case of need, can interpret the government's suggestions for better planting or care of animals, can adjust minor quarrels, can track down and return stolen animals, can count each herd or flock for tax purposes. Jordanians respect their police and there is a good relationship with law enforcement agencies.

European codes of law are based on punishing the wrongdoer, as an example to deter others. Arab tribal law, on the other hand, is based on compensation for wrong suffered. It is not a crime to steal camels from an enemy but it is a crime to steal them from a fellow tribesman. The loss must be compensated for or else the injured family may be in dire straits. The stolen camels may have been the family's sole means of support. Many acts illegal under Jordanian law are not considered illegal or immoral by tribal councils, using this yardstick.

There is no jury in Jordan so all cases are decided by a judge in open court. There is the progression of Magistrates' Courts, Courts of First Instance, Courts of Appeal, and the final High Court of Justice. These courts decide matters of law and fact in civil and criminal cases. Personal matters such as marriage, divorce, inheritance, and adoption are handled by special religious courts of Muslims or Christians.

The complex legal system reflects the diverse elements of Jordan society. There is the undergirding Islamic law and tribal custom. There is also the French code adopted by the Ottoman Turks and passed on by them to their subjects. During the mandate period, particularly on the West Bank, English common law prevailed. The present Jordanian legal system is a blend of these, adopting old laws to modern needs.

In 1957, when Sulaymen al-Nabulsi was Jordanian prime minister, top-ranking army officers and other politicians plotted to overthrow King Hussein. The plot was discovered in time for the king to enlist promises of aid from Iraq and Saudi Arabia. Forewarned by loyal Bedouin officers, Hussein drove the fifteen miles to Zarqa to turn back Bedouin regiments bound for Amman to avenge the reported death of their king. At the camp in Zarqa, Hussein visited the various headquarters and by personal appeals won the loyalty of all the regiments. The government was dismissed and martial law declared. Bedouin soldiers, their faces blackened with charcoal to show they meant business, patrolled the streets of the cities. Tank corps kept an eye on the disgruntled refugees. Political parties were banned.

The crisis seemed to unify Jordan in some intangible way and to define more clearly its relationships with the other Arab countries. In February, 1958, Egypt and Syria formed the United Arab Republic. Jordan and Iraq formed a federation, too, but it lasted only until July when a revolutionary mob killed King Feisal and dissolved the partnership. Egypt supported the Iraqi revolt and Jordan was left without close ties in the Arab world. At Hussein's request, British troops helped out in Jordan that summer much as American marines were helping Lebanon during the same period, and the United States started giving Jordan financial aid.

Jordan's meager natural resources make it imperative that Jordan get financial assistance from other countries. At the same time, help is seldom given without strings. This fact has made Jordan's foreign policy doubly difficult but in general Jordan's relations with the Arab world improved. King Hussein continued to work with other members of the Arab League. In 1955 Jordan was admitted to the United Nations. Jordan recognized the Yemen government backed by Egypt, resumed relations with Iraq in 1960, and recognized Syria after the United Arab Republic dissolved. King Hussein believed strongly in the importance of Arab unity and tried in a number of ways to make this a reality.

Jordan's political stability was tested in another way in 1961 when King Hussein married Toni Gardiner, daughter of a British colonel attached to the Jordan army. It was a love match, and Princess Muna, as she came to be called, was well received by the people. They have four children: Prince Abdullah, named for his great-grandfather; Prince Feisal; and the twins, Princess Zein and Princess Aisha. They live in one of several royal palaces, and the king commutes to his office by helicopter or automobile. The

King Hussein is proud of his family.

crown prince is not one of his sons, but Hussein's younger brother Hassan.

King Hussein enjoys driving fast cars and motorcycles and used to race in national sports-car events. He is an excellent pilot, frequently taking the controls on flights around the Arab world with his advisers, and he is adept at free-fall parachute jumping. His short stature, five feet four inches, is no handicap to his ability and daring. He is a fine horseman, a hunter, and a deep-sea fisherman. He introduced water-skiing to Jordan and enjoys it and scuba diving in the Gulf of Aqaba. His physical fitness and his love of danger are good qualities for a king who lives such a precarious life as King Hussein.

8

Conflicting Dreams

King Hussein believed strongly in the importance of Arab unity. He welcomed the series of Arab summit conferences from January, 1964, onward, and endorsed plans for a unified Arab military command. There were members of his government who disagreed with or mistrusted wholehearted cooperation. The policy of Arab unity in other countries suffered ups and downs, too, so that little more than talk had been accomplished by 1967. Arab countries agreed on the need for mutual support against Israeli aggression but the priority was less in those countries farther from Israel.

Jordan, however, was on the front line. The border with Israel had never been fixed and, in the intervening years since the 1948 war, the demilitarized zone was encroached on by skirmishes, raids, and reprisals. One everyday problem along the border was water. Armistice lines had often been drawn through villages, separating the village dwellers from their wells. Those excluded from Israel could look across and see others enjoying their harvest, and those without a well could see others benefiting. In general the Arabs had retained the less fertile highlands; if they had no water the land was useless. As time went on Jordan got new wells drilled in some of the villages, and other forms of livelihood developed in others.

Another problem was Israel's desire for more land as more Jews immigrated to Israel. Having been pushed out of their homes once, the Palestinians were very suspicious of further encroachments, whether nibbles or bites of land. Before partition the Zionists had proposed fantastic plans for diverting river waters to irrigate what became Israel. In the 1950's this plan was revived and Israel tried to achieve it by force. In 1956 Israel made an attempt, with support from Britain and France, to get more land to the south by taking over Sinai. The United States joined Egypt in thwarting this move. In the negotiations that followed, both Israel and Egypt were asked to accommodate a peace-keeping force to patrol the Gaza section and along the Straits of Tiran. Egypt accepted and Israel refused but the peace was kept for eleven years. On other borders, skirmishes continued. Harsh reprisals by the Israelis were repeatedly censured by the United Nations but no peaceful efforts were made.

During this period extremists, particularly in Egypt and Syria, made many reckless speeches on the national radio networks against each other and against King Hussein and against Israel. To a certain extent these were Arab bravado for the effect of the words meant little. But hot words often spark a fire unintentionally.

As a reprisal against increasing terrorist activities of the Palestinian Liberation Organization, Israel attacked the village of Samu in November, 1966. Samu was a village of four thousand Palestinian refugees, whom the Israelis accused of harboring terrorists from Syria. The Israeli army crossed the border near Hebron into Jordanian territory, dynamiting houses and the hospital. Israeli airplanes shot up the road so that the Jordan army was unable to rescue the villagers. The countries of the world were outraged, and the Security Council of the United Nations condemned Israel for the raid.

The following spring, 1967, a rumor of an Israeli military buildup spread through the Arab world. An air battle did occur with the Syrians in April over the Golan Heights. The Council of the Arab League met in Cairo to decide whether the Palestine Liberation Organization should launch attacks on Israel, bringing reprisals onto Jordan like Samu. The Chief of Staff of the Egyptian army was put in charge of a coordinated Arab military force. President Nasser of Egypt demanded the withdrawal of the United Nations Emergency Force from Gaza. When the Secretary-General of the United Nations did as Nasser asked, he also ordered the force to leave Sharm el Sheikh, the station for guarding the Straits of Tiran. Freedom of shipping in these straits was important both for Jordan to get to its port of Aqaba and for Israel to get to its port of Eilat. Egypt felt within her rights to block Israeli ships from using the straits and to close the Suez Canal to Israeli ships. Israel was again asked to put the United Nations Force on her side of the border and again Israel refused.

King Hussein was sure the situation was sliding into war. On May 30, 1967, he flew to Cairo to confer with President Nasser. King Hussein put aside all the insults from Radio Cairo, and the difficult predicaments created for him by the Palestine Liberation Organization. He begged President Nasser again to use his prestige to get the Arab countries together. King Hussein knew that all Arabs, to the Israelis, were lumped together as a single enemy. Jordan would be in the direct line of fire. Hussein and Nasser did sign a military pact to defend each other in case of enemy attack, and Egyptian General Riad went to Jordan to direct and coordinate Arab armies.

Both Egypt and Jordan had declared a state of emergency, and troops were given special orders in case of attack. They asked for and got promises of military assistance from Saudi Arabia, Syria, and Iraq. Early in the morning of June 5, with the Arabs still getting ready, Israel bombed Egyptian air bases and crippled the Egyptian Air Force, reminiscent of the Japanese attack on Pearl Harbor in December, 1941. The Jordanians, because of their pact with Egypt, flew across to Israel, found no planes but bombed the airstrips, and flew home to refuel. The Israeli planes caught the Jordanian Air Force on the ground and destroyed it in one raid. Without air cover in the open terrain of Jordan there was no protection for tanks and soldiers. Bit by bit the Israeli Air Force put these forces out of action.

That afternoon, with precision flying, the Israeli flyers flew at the king's palace and machine-gunned Hussein's office at point-blank range. The king was at the army headquarters, however, or else he would surely have been killed. The next night, June 6, the United Nations ordered an immediate and unconditional cease-fire. The Jordanians tried to keep the positions they held, and the Israelis tried to beat the Jordanians back with increased action. The Jordanians fought desperately for Jerusalem, but they were defeated by midday on June 7, and on the morning of June 8, Jordan accepted the Security Council's cease-fire.

King Hussein was with his troops on the front, or visiting them in first-aid tents, or working out the next move at the command headquarters. He did not sleep at all during those three days. General Riad was still in command, but he had very poor communications with Egypt and was not told the truth about the heavy losses suffered by the Egyptian army. The troops came from Iraq, but the Saudi Arabian forces did not arrive until the battles were all finished, and the Syrians kept postponing their support and did not help out even after they had arrived.

The king said in summary:

One of our basic mistakes in the June conflict was not tailoring our operations to our resources and leaving aside all help from the outside. We held to the principle of protecting Arab strategic interests in general while reducing our own to a secondary level. As a result, since we had counted on help from allies who, for one reason or another, failed to honor their agreements, we were forced as the operation ran its course to improvise with the means we had available at the moment. Most of the time, our means turned out to be less than we had counted on and insufficient for our needs to oppose the enemy's tactics.

With defeat, Jordan had to reassess its geographic and strategic situation. Jordan had lost the West Bank to occupying forces, and most of its military potential had been destroyed. King Hussein revised Jordan's defense to take into account the enemy power, and what a limited action with reduced air power can achieve against this. Jordan had never had an offensive army, merely one of defense, but the June battles had showed the Jordan army its weaknesses and limitations.

As far as King Hussein was concerned, the June, 1967, conflict was another battle in the long-term, unending fight with Israel. Hussein flew again to Cairo to confer with President Nasser. They tried to prepare a workable solution to present to the United Nations, but Arab extremists clouded the proposals. The Arabs said they would agree to recognize everyone's rights to live in the area under dispute, to end warfare, and to reopen the Suez Canal to all nations if the Israelis would withdraw from the territories they occupied as of June and would allow the Palestinian refugees to return or be compensated.

Not all the Arab world supported this peace proposal, some

thinking it did not go far enough. The important factor was that Jordan and Egypt had agreed upon it, the two countries who had fought and lost the most, and they were willing to negotiate on its terms. Little world press coverage was given to this statement. Part of the mechanism of Israel is its direct tie with World Zionism, and this gives Israel automatic affiliation with the 16 million Jews scattered around the world. Whatever Israel says gets instantly spread and printed, in newspapers everywhere. The Arabs have no comparable "press service." People believed that the Jewish side of the case was the whole story, and King Hussein found it difficult to make his viewpoint heard or understood.

On June 26, 1967, King Hussein addressed the United Nations General Assembly. With great fervor he explained:

> I can very well imagine the hue and cry that would have arisen had the Arabs attacked first, and how bitter would be the denunciations if we were today in Tel Aviv. Why this double standard on the part of some Powers in considering the rights of the Arabs and the rights of the Israelis? We know, of course, that world sympathy for the Jews created Israel in the first place. But world sympathy for a tragic past does not permit condoning aggressive acts on the part of those who were once the victims of aggression.
>
> I will not speak to you only about peace, for the precondition of peace is justice. When we have achieved justice we will have achieved peace in the Middle East.

These were not just words, they were the cornerstone of the continuing Arab policy. This is what the Arabs had asked for before the Mandate, during the Mandate, in appeals before partition, and many times since 1948. The only thing the rest of the world had been able to offer was a United Nations force to super-

King Hussein confers with former Secretary-General of the United Nations, U Thant.

vise the borders, assistance for the refugees, and armaments to escalate the danger of general war. When Israel had been weak, in the 1950's, it had not wanted peace nor would it agree to negotiations offered by Egypt. When the Israelis were victorious they would not be generous, or heed the basic lesson. Their security would never be assured until they learned to live with the Arabs.

On November 22, 1967, the United Nations passed unanimously a resolution affirming respect for the territorial integrity and political independence of every state in the area, requesting withdrawal of Israeli armed forces from territories of recent conflict, guaranteeing freedom of navigation, achieving a just settlement of the refugee problem, and guaranteeing peace with demilitarized zones. A special representative of the secretary-general was designated to investigate and report on the situation, and from that day to this, Special Envoy Gunnar Jarring, a Swede, has had this assignment.

"A settlement of the refugee problem" has been basic to all negotiation with Israel, and has been stated and restated at the United Nations. It started with Palestinians fleeing from fighting in 1948, fleeing from neighbors suddenly turned enemies, fleeing from foster brothers. In Jerusalem it was the custom for two male children born in the same neighborhood at about the same time, one Jewish and one Arab, to be nursed by each other's mothers and become "foster brothers." The wealth or poverty of the families was of no consequence for this custom, and from that day forward the families shared special occasions, exchanged gifts and condolences, and did all the occasional things that indicate "friends of the family." The refugees fled not permanently but simply to get out of the line of fire. They did not know where the boundaries of partition were, but the better organized and more desperate Israelis did, and the fleeing Palestinians were often encouraged to leave an area or their villages were destroyed on their heels. The Israelis needed land and they did not want to have an Arab majority in their new Jewish homeland. The Palestinians refused to accept compensation for their property when they were prevented from returning, saying that they should be allowed the option to return. They wanted the right to choose, not to be forced to accept a money settlement.

During the fighting in 1967 there was another flight to the East Bank, and some Palestinians became refugees for the second time.

The Jericho camp was totally abandoned and new camps had to be set up on the East Bank. Those who remained behind faced a wide assortment of hardships and harassment, some were locked up in their houses for long periods and others were not allowed to collect food on their own farms. In the new camps, that first winter, tents were in short supply and many that did arrive blew away or were inadequate against the snow. As quickly as possible schools were started again and medical services resumed.

As in 1948, the human problems were overshadowed by political indecision. In spite of more than a dozen United Nations agencies dealing with the Middle East situation, in one way or another, and in spite of the unanimous approval given in the Security Council to issues for negotiation, no one was willing to exert the special pressure to hammer out an agreement. As in 1948, the real losers in the conflict with Israel were the Palestinians. Jordan was disillusioned by the scant help she had gotten from the other Arab countries. The commandos, or *fedayeen,* had not mobilized their forces at all, although the leader of the Palestine Liberation Organization, Ahmed Shukairy, was given the go-ahead by the Arab League.

From the beginning the Arab League was committed to helping the Palestinians gain independence, preferably by peaceful means. For almost twenty years this continued to be the policy. In 1964 the League gave permission and money for a Palestinian Liberation Organization army. By mid-1970 this force numbered ten thousand troops. Not all Palestinians liked the Palestinian Liberation Organization (PLO) or its leadership. Another group, *Al-Fatah,* rallied to the leadership of Yasir Arafat. Its fifteen thousand recruits were sponsored entirely by private Palestinians channeling payments through the governments of Saudi Arabia, Kuwait, Libya, and Abu Dhabi. Neither group has any aim other

Palestinian refugees crossed the Jordan River on the badly damaged Allenby Bridge in July 1967 to resettle in East Jordan.

than freeing Palestine to set up a democratic state with freedom of religion.

There are ten other groups of fedayeen, some splinters from Al-Fatah or PLO and others representing different political viewpoints or sponsors. One of these, the Popular Front for the Liberation of Palestine, is led by George Habash. He got interested in the philosophy of revolt when he was in college, and as a Palestinian he saw a practical application for his theories. For a long time he was a doctor in Amman and then in Damascus. After the

1967 conflict with Israel, Habash began full-time work with the resistance.

During the last week of March, 1968, the Israelis attacked the village of Shuna, north of the Dead Sea. By this time Jordan had reorganized its army and was prepared. The army fought the Israelis in a positive, organized, efficient way and disabled many Israeli tanks. The village was leveled, but the Israelis were repulsed. At the same time Israel took "police action" against Karameh, a Palestinian refugee camp administered by UNRWA. The Jordanians had evacuated the twenty-five thousand inhabitants, fearing an attack, so all the Israelis could do was dynamite every house. The fedayeen arrived and helped the Jordan army fight, but they did not obey army commands. King Hussein was very angry, because fedayeen raids had provoked the Israeli attacks on Shuna and Karameh. When a mass funeral was held in Amman for all the dead the king was uneasy to see many commandos, in their leopard-spotted uniforms and toting their submachine guns, marching in the procession.

Hussein knew that to force a showdown with the fedayeen his army would have to fight in many parts of the country. This would mean civil war. The king tried first to work the matter out diplomatically between the disagreeing factions in his own cabinet. Jordan's prime minister at that time was Bahjat al-Talhouny, and he opposed restricting fedayeen activities. The other political leader was Wasfi al-Tell who did not trust either the Palestinians or President Nasser of Egypt.

Other Arab countries criticized King Hussein for trying to make the commandos obey him, and they sent guns and money to the fedayeen. From Jordan went the commandos on their raids into Israel, and the Israeli retaliation was made into Jordanian territory. How tolerant could a host government afford to be? The king summed up the situation by saying: "If there is anybody who thinks he is a better Arab nationalist than I, let him demonstrate it in his own country and not by using Jordan as his proving ground."

In February, 1969, all the fedayeen groups sent representatives to a conference in Cairo to coordinate their activities. Yasir Arafat, of Al-Fatah, was chosen chairman. The conference decided, in direct opposition to King Hussein, that a diplomatic settlement with Israel would compromise the overall future of Palestine. King Hussein had also told the commando council that they must abide by Jordanian laws in return for his not interfering in their

Jordanians line a street in Amman for a military parade.

activities. The fedayeen were asked not to carry guns or to wear their uniforms in Jordanian towns, to carry identification cards and use Jordanian license plates, and to recognize the authority of Jordanian justice in crimes. The fedayeen leaders agreed to these rules.

The commandos were recruited in the refugee camps, among the young men and women who felt the future was bleak for them if not hopeless. The Palestinians in the camps have a particular love for their land which is difficult to measure. They were the farmers who were not employable anywhere else or in other sorts of jobs. Their children are better educated, thanks to the elementary and vocational schools of UNRWA, and they are disciplined and purposeful. The second generation refugees are more aware of the rest of the world than their parents, and they want to participate in it. If possible, they want to get training and put it to use on a job. For those with no other alternatives, dying on a guerrilla mission is better than the living death of the refugee camp.

While the camps bred guerrillas, the Jordanians on the West Bank continued to suffer from the occupation. In March, 1969, the United Nations Human Rights Commission accused Israel of continued violation of human rights in the occupied territories, including "acts of destroying homes of the Arab civilian population, deportation of inhabitants and the resorting to violence against inhabitants expressing their resentment of occupation." The Arabs realize that in order to be a potential home for all the Jews in the world, it is necessary for Israel to have an increasing amount of land, preferably in Palestine. Israeli colonization has included the practice of expelling the people who originally lived there, whether it be by using the terrorist tactics of the Stern and Irgun gangs of the 1940's, or by government policies preventing

Palestinians from returning to their land. There are severe limits and rules imposed by the military governors which make it impossible for ordinary Palestinians to lead normal lives or plan for the future.

Later in 1969 a British observer reported the measures used by the Israelis including deportation, destruction of homes, imprisonment, torture, curfews, and the encouragement of Arab departure from the territories, and: "There seems to be virtual unanimity in the occupied territories that the only help is self-help, and that this means force." Yasir Arafat echoed this viewpoint when he said: "We can lose two, three, four times over. The Israelis can only lose once. We have lost our homes, our farms, our dignity, our identity, our humanity. All we have (striking the butt of his rifle) is this."

Widespread fighting broke out in Amman in June, 1970, between the army, angered by the commandos who were not abiding by Hussein's rules, and the fedayeen, equally angered by the handicaps these rules put on their operations. Syria supported the commandos; Libya and Egypt pleaded for a cease-fire. A four-man mediation team was sent by the Arab League, made up of men from Egypt, Libya, Sudan, and Algeria, to arbitrate the dispute. Negotiations failed. In September three international airliners were hijacked by the commandos, taken to the Jordanian desert, and the passengers held hostage for guerrilla prisoners in several countries. Fierce clashes along the fedayeen supply routes, in Irbid, Zarqa, Salt, and Marfaq, spread the fighting into civil war. There were severe shortages of water, electricity failure, and lack of food and medicines. Army firepower leveled two refugee camps that were commando strongholds. The Arab League was very angry, and their four-man committee finally arranged another cease-fire late in the month. King Hussein was summoned to Cairo for talks with President Nasser and other Arab leaders. Nasser managed to cool tempers, and then he died the next day.

In human terms the civil war was brutal and devastating. The International Red Cross estimated six thousand dead and eight thousand wounded. Whole sections of Amman were destroyed and entire villages lay in ruins. Upwards of one hundred thousand were made homeless. King Hussein had told his military government to "cope with the situation with appropriate effort, firmness and fortitude to restore security, and order and stability." The brutality of the response, on both sides, was an indication of the totally frustrating situation. No one emerged the winner, and reactions around the Arab world ranged from cutting off subsidies to Jordan's treasury by Kuwait and Libya, to unkept promises by Iraq to help the Palestinians. For the first time the commandos called for the overthrow of King Hussein as a stepping stone to transforming Israel into a Palestinian state.

The truce supervisors scuttled from one cease-fire violation to another, all over the country. In December another agreement was reached, but sporadic fighting continued. King Hussein formed a new cabinet with Wasfi al-Tell as prime minister, and he was told by the king to "deal conclusively and without hesitation with the plotters who want to establish a separate Palestinian state and destroy the unity of Jordanian and Palestinian people." The commandos responded by a sabotage campaign against the Jordanian economy, including blowing up the pipeline at Zarqa, blasting bridges and rail lines, mining public roads, attacking the phosphate mines, and handicapping repairs on the East Ghor canal.

By mid-June, 1971, Prime Minister al-Tell reported the army had rounded up 2,300 commandos and banned the Popular Front for the Liberation of Palestine from the country. He said commandos loyal to Jordan would be free to continue raiding Israel, but that those plotting against Jordan itself would be imprisoned or deported. The commando reply was to murder Wasfi al-Tell in Cairo in November after another round of negotiations had broken down.

9

Jerusalem, Holy City

One of the thorniest problems in the Middle East today is what to do about Jerusalem. Under the terms of the 1947 United Nations partition, Jerusalem was to be an international city. But by the time the fighting had stopped, the Zionists held the new part of Jerusalem, where many wealthy Arabs lived, and the Arabs held the Old City which was as holy to them as to anyone else. Its crenellated walls and towers are all that distinguish it now from the surrounding modern city, which since 1967 has been joined again to it.

Jerusalem is perched on the hills of ancient Judea some 2,600 feet above sea level. The city enjoys a healthy climate: a sprinkling of snow in winter, and in the summer, breezes to relieve the heat. The Old City is essentially a medieval town, with narrow twisted streets and wide flights of shallow steps to account for the hills on which Jerusalem is built. Instead of having a castle at the center, there is the temple area on its large raised stone platform —sacred to three great faiths: Christianity, Islam, and Judaism. The dominant building is the Dome of the Rock with its golden dome. Also on the platform are the al-Aqsa mosque, the Islamic Museum, and many lesser buildings which are remnants of Roman temples and other holy shrines.

The eastern wall of the Old City of Jerusalem edges the raised temple area.

The marble and mosaic bands of the Dome of the Rock are a colorful base for the golden dome.

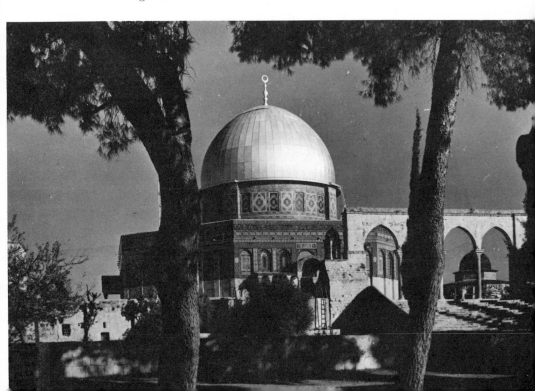

sacred temple area are the Muslim, Arab Chris-
and Jewish quarters of the city, overflowing with
se families have lived in the Old City for centuries
th new arrivals who want to live in this holy spot. From
st inside the St. Stephen's gate winds a series of streets called
the Via Dolorosa, believed by Christians to be the route Jesus
took, when he entered the city after praying in the Garden of
Gethsemane, to his crucifixion. At many points along the way are
places where incidents occurred during Christ's walk with the

The Via Dolorosa leads
to the Holy Sepulchre,
Jerusalem.

cross, called "Stations of the Cross." When medieval pilgrims returned to Europe and tried to describe the Via Dolorosa to their
fellow worshippers, they often built a small replica of the holy
walk in cathedral gardens. From this custom came the Stations of
the Cross in present-day Catholic churches.

The street winds past churches and markets, under archways
and around corners, its cobblestoned course leading to the
Church of the Holy Sepulchre. Every Friday at three the Francis-
cans lead a procession along this "street of sorrows," stopping at
each station to pray. Some stations have been established by archeological excavation as authentic, although the Jerusalem of
Jesus' day is twenty feet below the present street level. Other stations are honored by traditional pilgrim veneration. To relive the
original procession, one must remember that it was a Roman city
with Pilate's office and courtyard near the present city gate, public baths where a chapel now stands, and many Roman houses,
shops, and flights of steps leading up the hill to the open place for
crucifying criminals. At Eastertime these events are acted out
with more ceremony, and group after group of pilgrims carry a
cross into the church.

The last five stations of the cross are inside the Church of the
Holy Sepulchre, making it the holiest church in Christendom.
The church has been damaged and rebuilt many times since
Queen Helena built the first church. The interior is a confusing
cluster of chapels jealously guarded by various sects. Services follow one another throughout the day, incense burns, and
hundreds of lamps smoke with feeble light. Amid the hubbub of
continuous chanting, the feeling of reverence, the services of worship in many languages, the focal point is the tomb site covered
with a marble slab worn down by the lips of fervent worshippers.
As Mark Twain remarked: "When one stands where the Savior

e finds it all he can do to keep it strictly before his
: was not crucified in a Catholic church."

e winter of 1964 Pope Paul VI visited the Holy
Muslims and Jews, as well as Christians of all denomina-
ns, united to give him welcome. The event was covered by
press and television so that most of the world shared in the historic event. Millions had an opportunity to see Jerusalem with
their own eyes. Like actual pilgrims to Jerusalem, what they saw
was only the tip of an iceberg of religious history.

The original city was a Jebusite fortress on a rocky hill. This
made a natural wall on all but the north side, where man-made
walls were needed for defense. During the time of Solomon the
city was extended considerably to the west, to another ridge, and
to the north enclosed a threshing floor where David had built an
altar. On this rocky shelf Solomon built a temple.

Two hundred years elapsed before another major addition was
made to the city walls, and in doing so Hezekiah enclosed land
lying between the original city and Solomon's westward "upper
city." The only water supply for the city was a spring outside the
walls to the east. Threatened with a siege by the Assyrians, the
king ordered a long tunnel to be cut underground into the city.
The source outside was sealed up.

Frantic haste must have been employed. One group of men
started from the spring, and the others started digging from the
inside of the city. They sought the softer stone in the core of the
hill, feeling their way, making an irregular opening two feet wide
and fourteen feet high in some places. Miraculously, the two work
parties met. The quarter-mile-long tunnel is still open today, with
spring water flowing through it, and the hasty workmanship evident. For many centuries the Pool of Siloam, into which the
spring water emptied, was a public laundry place.

Succeeding kings enclosed more land to the north, particularly during the Roman period of prosperity. The city was fought over by many, including the rival Seleucids of Antioch and the Ptolemies in Alexandria. The Romans captured Jerusalem in 63 B.C. and made the city part of their empire. Herod, of Arab stock but Jewish religion, was one of the greatest rulers during this period. He built a huge tower, carved out of living rock, which became one of three to guard his new palace. He built another tower, at a corner of the temple area, which controlled both domestic riots in the temple area and the strategic defense of the city. It was a fortress, palace, and prison in one.

Herod built the temple that Jesus knew. In order to enlarge the area, Herod leveled the top of the hill and constructed a temple area on top of the rock platform. He intended it to be larger than the Acropolis in Athens, and he succeeded. The enclosure is thirty-five acres in all. On the southern corners were vaulted substructures, storage chambers that can still be inspected. Herod surrounded the enclosure with porticoes and built the temple itself on a raised platform of stone. In this tranquil and beautiful place Jesus spoke on many subjects and quoted the Prophet Isaiah: "My house shall be called of all nations the house of prayer."

Herod's grandson Agrippa built another city wall, farther north, and enclosing for the first time the spot where Jesus was crucified. He built the handsome Damascus gate, rebuilt by Hadrian, and clearly shown in the mosaic floor found at Madaba. The temple was destroyed in A.D. 70 in a revolt against the Romans but the western foundation survived. It is revered today by Jews as the Wailing Wall. Eventually Hadrian rebuilt the city in pagan Roman style and erected a temple to Jupiter in the sacred enclosure. On the site of the crucifixion he built a temple to

Venus, which helped Constantine's mother, Empress Helena, to identify the spot where she came to Jerusalem to build churches commemorating Christ's life.

After Constantine declared Christianity the new state religion, he called the Council of Nicea in A.D. 325. The purpose was to draw up a uniform creed for all Christians. During the nearly three hundred years of Christian expansion, regional differences of interpretation developed. Basically the conflict was the difference in Hellenic and Semitic concepts of the Trinity. The eastern Semitic churches reluctantly accepted the Nicene Creed, because eastern culture traditionally put the Father as head of the family and the Son subservient to Him.

By the time Byzantine Emperor Marcian called the Council of Chalcedon in A.D. 451, he was powerful enough as a leader to expel those churches reluctant to accept the doctrine of the Trinity. Known as the Monophysites, believing in the oneness of God, they found a warm reception among the Assyrians and the Persians. Their present-day followers, forming many sects, add to the color and confusion of life in Jerusalem.

The Syriacs are one of these, more commonly called Nestorians after their fourth-century patriarch, Nestorius. Their ritual is still in the Aramaic language spoken by Christ. They were energetic missionaries who established churches along the Great Caravan Route as far as China. Marco Polo mentions seeing their churches on his journey to visit the Great Khan in the late thirteenth century. They are also spoken of as Jacobites, after the active missionary bishop, Jacob Baradaeus. There are about two hundred thousand members scattered throughout the Middle East.

The Armenians claim to be the first kingdom outside of Byzantium to have adopted Christianity as the official religion. The Armenian peoples have been buffeted by many conquerors, but their church liturgy and literature have helped preserve both a spiritual and national unity. One of their patriarchs is resident in Jerusalem.

The Copts are the Christians of Egypt, Nubia, and Ethiopia. It was the Coptic church that sparked the monastic movement in the third century. Monasteries dotted the deserts of southern Egypt and Nubia. From there the idea of retreating from the world spread to Sinai, Jordan, Syria, and finally to Europe.

The Greek Orthodox church is organized on national lines. A Metropolitan in each country is head of that church. Consequently he is more of a politician than a practicing prelate. Orthodox churches, although centered in the Middle East, are scattered in other countries from Finland to Japan and in North and South America.

Most of these Eastern churches have, at one time or another, split up and parts have affiliated with the Papacy in Rome. These are called Uniate churches, or "Latins," a term used from Crusader times, to distinguish them from the more independent eastern churches. All these many churchmen, in their distinctive dress and with their monastic orders, have attached themselves to holy sites in and around Jerusalem.

The Western and Eastern churches have long used different calendars, the Eastern churches holding their traditional services twelve days later than the Western. There is a movement now to consolidate the festivals according to the Western calendar, but this revision of the calendar has not been accepted in Jordan. It is probably just as well, because if all the sects celebrated on the same days, the resulting crush of people would be overwhelming. Even today, with the churches following two calendars, the crowding of participants in the holy places is often unbearable. This is particularly true in the Church of the Holy Sepulchre where the

A Greek baptism occurs in the Jordan River at the spot where Christ was baptized.

lack of ventilation is acute. The heavy incense, smoking lamps, packed humanity, and succession of services exhaust the air and leave one faint.

All the churches were destroyed in 614 when the Persians captured Jerusalem and massacred thousands of its Christian inhabitants. Fourteen years later Heraclius recaptured Jerusalem and, because the Jewish inhabitants had welcomed the Persians, he killed many of them. By the time Muhammed came to the city a few years later, it was a shambles. This did not matter, because it was a miraculous journey from Mecca on a mysterious winged animal and escorted by the angel Gabriel. Like many other religious experiences, it was difficult for Muhammed to describe his vision in everyday terms. He made a temporary ascent to Heaven from the rock in the former temple area, making Jerusalem more sacred to Muslims than simply as the city of the Jewish prophets and of Jesus, whom they also revere.

Jerusalem, which was at that time called by its Roman name Aelia, was captured by the Muslim Caliph Omar in 638. He cleared much of the rubble in the temple area with his bare hands. There were no traces left of Jewish or pagan temples, and the rock over which the Dome was eventually built was under a rubbish heap. It was no longer consecrated ground but Omar directed that it be cleansed and prayers said when it had been purified. Many caliphs who followed after him had their leadership proclaimed there, and it was the religious capital of Islam during periods when rival groups controlled Mecca and Medina. It was *al-Quds,* "the Holy City," as Muslims call it to this day.

Where Omar had first put a makeshift mosque, the al-Aqsa mosque was built. Nearby was the rock where Muhammed had had his vision. This was the rock the Jebusites used for threshing, a high place where the wind could scatter the chaff and where the grain could be stored in a cave below. It was the rock on which David built an altar, and Solomon, a temple. Tradition maintains that in earlier history it was also the rock on which Abraham prepared to sacrifice his son Isaac. Over this rock a shrine was built, called the Dome of the Rock. The area became known as *al-Haram al-Sharif,* or "the noble sanctuary." It was equal in merit as a place of pilgrimage to Mecca and Medina, and many pilgrims go each year to pray there. Successive caliphs further beautified Jerusalem, or built another mosque, or endowed a school. The pursuit of learning was considered a religious duty by Muslims, and in medieval times Jerusalem was a center for Muslim scholars as it is today for all three faiths.

Built by Byzantine craftsmen, the Dome of the Rock is octagonal in plan with four simple entrances. Two concentric rows of columns form the circular aisles inside. The inner circle of columns supports the dome, which is fifty feet in diameter and one hundred feet high, a double dome like the later ones of St. Peter's Cathedral in Rome and St. Paul's in London. The inner dome is painted, as are the tie beams that connect the columns. The circular scheme is also used in the windows of colored glass and the inscriptions that run continuously around the lower edge of the

The rock within the Dome of the Rock is a rough contrast to the delicate arched colonnade.

dome. In the sixteenth century the exterior was faced with tiles above a band of marble, and these tiles give the Dome of the Rock its shimmering color and beauty.

The building has been badly damaged a number of times by earthquake, conquest, neglect, and fire, but much of the original remains. Many of the interior mosaics and some of the tiles over the upper half of the exterior are original, as are all but two of the marble columns. Israeli mortar fire in 1948 damaged the Dome of the Rock so extensively that it required complete restoration. All the Muslim nations contributed to a fund for repairs, inside and out. The 200-ton lead-covered dome was replaced by one of aluminum bronze alloy, some 160 tons lighter. Originally the dome was gilded copper but not since the eleventh century, when the copper was replaced by lead, has it shone like gold. The restorations were completed early in August, 1964. King Hussein, together with Muslim and Christian dignitaries from all the Arab nations, reopened the beautiful shrine. Indirect lighting inside and floodlights outside illuminate the richly decorated building and the new golden dome. It still shines in the heart of Jerusalem, dominating the Old City with its beauty.

In 969 the caliphs of Egypt became Jerusalem's rulers, and in 1071 the Seljuk Turks conquered Byzantium and took over Palestine. It was their raids on the Christian pilgrim routes that prompted the Crusades. The Crusaders were lords of Jerusalem for less than a hundred years, the longest period extending from 1099 to 1187. After Saladin had defeated the Crusaders, he restored the al-Aqsa mosque and built two new religious schools, hostels for scholars, and a hospital. At spots traditionally associated with Muhammed's visit to the city, other wealthy men endowed land as religious foundations. A foundation is in Arabic called a waqf, and it administers funds for pious purposes. Many of these foundations still operate today.

The Arabs were tolerant of the other religious faiths. After Saladin had recaptured Jerusalem, he kept the pilgrim routes open for Christians. Muslim pilgrims continued to flock to Jerusalem, too, because, unlike the pilgrimage to Mecca, there is no fixed date or year for a pilgrimage to Jerusalem. There was a small flow of Jewish refugees from Christian Europe to the more tolerant lands of Islam. A fraction of these went to Palestine and settled in Jerusalem. From time to time they made trouble for the governors, but the Arabs were generally indulgent to the tiny standoffish minority.

The Mamelukes from Egypt took over the city in 1247 and ruled for almost three hundred years. Many fine mosques and buildings were built during that period. Suleiman the Magnificent, who consolidated the Ottoman empire which conquered Jerusalem in the sixteenth century, succeeded to the title "servant and guardian" of the holy places of Mecca, Medina, and Jerusalem. He carried on extensive repairs to the Dome of the Rock and other buildings in the area, installed a new water system including five fountains in the Haram area, and continued the practice of endowing hostels and religious schools. He also built the superstructure of the present walls of the Old City.

In 1948 the United Nations provided in the Partition Agreement for an international Jerusalem, to free the holy places from political controversy. When fighting broke out after the partition plan was announced, the Old City of Jerusalem was protected and defended successfully by the Arabs. As they had for centuries, the Muslim families of Jerusalem continued to take care of the holy shrines of all faiths. The Jordan government allocated a portion of its meager funds for repairs and conservation, to preserve the historic tranquility of the Old City. When an equally brave defense of the city was made by the Arabs in 1967 and they were defeated, the Israelis said they were "liberating" the city. Jerusalem is no longer divided by a "no-man's-land," to be sure, but the unique character of the Old City is being destroyed.

As soon as the June, 1967, conflict was over, the Old City, re-named East Jerusalem, was connected with the electric and tele-phone lines of new Jerusalem, and the lines with the rest of occu-pied Jordan severed. This violated international law and cut the Arabs in Jerusalem off from all their compatriots. The Israelis also started immediately to develop the Old City: buildings were razed so that for the first time cars and buses could drive into the Old City; slum clearance evicted six thousand Arab people to make way for six hundred Jewish families; nine high-rise hotels were built, and sixteen more are planned, to ring the Old City.

The United States has protested, the United Nations has pro-tested, and many Arab governments have protested to Israel. So have the Pope and other Christian leaders. Jerusalem's Israeli mayor, Teddy Kollek, replies that Israel has an unshakable right "to build a good city for all the citizens of Jerusalem regardless of future boundaries and as befits good city planning." There is lit-tle international support for Israel's city planning. The Jerusalem master plan extends greater Jerusalem to the occupied towns of Nablus on the north and Bethlehem on the south, making it five hundred times the size of the present walled city. To provide for the population density of such a plan, it will be necessary to bring industry into the city and to build new housing for the 50 percent of the immigrants to Israel who want to live in Jerusa-lem.

Arabs whose families have lived in Jerusalem for hundreds of years see what their families preserved being "modernized" for tourist expediency. They see Israelis extending the city limits so that there will be a Jewish majority, and all Arab historical associations with the city will disappear. Like the rest of Palestine, the Arabs fear Jerusalem will be swallowed up in the Zionist version of progress.

King Hussein, in an unusual Easter message in 1971, appealed to the world:

> The Holy City of Christians, Muslims and Jews has been occupied forcibly by a State and Government which claims to represent all Jewry and pretends that Jerusalem belongs more to them than it does either to the Christian or Muslim world. This State and Government has annexed Jerusalem against repeated resolutions of the United Nations. None of the Great Powers, including Great Britain and the United States, has recognized Israel's annexation of the Arab city or the contention that it is their capital. Nonetheless Israel continues to defy the feelings and wishes of the whole world. They disregard and violate the rights of the Arab population and the religious sensibilities of over 700,000,000 Muslims.

10

All Roads Lead to Amman

When Emir Abdullah selected Amman as his capital in 1922 he had little choice. Jerusalem, the traditional capital, was the administrative center of the British-controlled mandate of Palestine. The village of some three thousand people had the one advantage of a fairly central location, but the Emir and his retinue had to live in tents for over a year. It proved a difficult task to build a capital city in a constricted network of wadis. Of necessity the city has had to overflow onto the surrounding plateau. It is now the population center of the country with almost half a million inhabitants.

Modern Amman has rapidly outgrown its rather simple origins. Although the site was occupied in Paleolithic times, probably on account of the abundant springs—many chipped-stone tools attest the fact—it comes into recorded history about 1200 B.C. as Rabbath Ammon, chief city of the kings of Ammon.

The Bible mentions that David ordered Uriah the Hittite to lead the attack on the town in order to cause Uriah's death, thus making it possible for David to marry his widow Bathsheba. The town was known for its wealth and wickedness, and its destruction was foretold by the prophets Amos, Jeremiah, and Ezekiel. In the third century B.C. the Ptolemic king Philadelphus cap-

Amman's center is a blend of old and new.

tured the city from the Greeks and renamed it for himself, Philadelphia. Under the Roman rulers that followed, it became a
member city of the Decapolis. The only large Roman ruin surviving and still being used today is an amphitheater built against
one hill. It was dedicated to Hadrian in A.D. 129. Audiences of six
thousand can still sit on the tiered seats and watch dance festivals,
concerts, dramas, and prizefights.

Atop one of the seven hills is a citadel with remnants of many
historical periods. It was built on a rocky plateau and protected
by natural valleys except on the north. The fortress had towers at
the corners for defense, and a rock wall to the north. In the central courtyard a temple was built during Aurelius's reign, honoring Hercules. The Byzantines built a new gate for the citadel

when they used it, and the Omayyads made it a more comfortable spot by adding a castle alongside.

Amman flourished as a Christian city, as the seat of the bishopric of Petra and Philadelphia. Later it was a link on the caravan route from Damascus to Mecca. When the caliphate moved from Damascus to Baghdad, Amman lost its importance. It did not recapture it until recent times, when King Abdullah built the new capital to provide for the expanding functions of government. The Arab-Israeli wars have compounded the city's growing pains. The city has absorbed refugees on each occasion, and has had to administer an increasing number of social services for them. A city plan, adopted in 1955, has slowly removed the worst traffic snarls, and builders have been encouraged to spread out onto the surrounding plateau. The older houses sprawl up the sides of the seven hills. Small stores specializing in wares of one sort or another, all competing tradesmen clustered together, are in the *suq,*

Amman's Roman theater is evidence of the town's antiquity.

or main bazaar. There isn't an adequate bus service, so many people get around in taxis, or in taxis called *services* in which one can buy a single seat.

The administrative offices cluster around Basman Palace in a new quarter of the city. The Council of Representatives has a handsome new building. Waving over it is the flag of Jordan representing both the long history of Islamic rule and the king's tie to Mecca. His family were the custodians of the holy city for many generations, because Muhammed was a member of the Hashem family in the Kuraish tribe. King Hussein is a descendant of the Hashems. The flag has three even stripes: black, at the top, for the Abbasid Caliphate of Baghdad; white for the Omayyads of Damascus; green, at the bottom, for the Alids of Kerbela (Persia). At the hoist is a red chevron for the Berbers of North Africa, and in the center is an irregular seven-pointed white star for the Hashemite family.

When the Hashemite Kingdom of Jordan came into being in 1950, it inherited the government established in 1946 when Transjordan became fully independent. This was a hereditary monarchy and a two-branch legislature. The Council of Representatives is elected, only adult males voting, and the Council of Notables is appointed by the king. Palestinians have equal rights and representation if they accept Jordanian citizenship, and there are always a few Palestinians in the Cabinet. Each of the eight liwas has a governor who is responsible to the minister of interior. Each town is managed by an elected mayor and town council. The governor of the district has the power to veto the elected officials if necessary for good government.

Half of the voting districts are west of the Jordan River and at present under Israeli occupation. Recently the Israelis have allowed the publication of a daily newspaper in Arabic, but the two dailies published in Amman circulate only in East Jordan. They are *al-Difa's* (Defense) and *al-Dustur* (Constitution). There are also four weekly newspapers and about twenty magazines published in Amman. Some are monthly and some quarterly, ranging from journals for farmers or lawyers or engineers to poetry, medical news, and sports activities. Newspapers and magazines have poor circulation outside Amman, and many people depend on radio.

Jordan's first radio transmitter was in Ramallah, but one was built in Amman for better East Bank transmission and now that is used exclusively. The Israelis use the other one for Arabic-language broadcasts in Israel and the occupied territories. Radio Jordan programs include music, news, editorial comment, readings from the Koran, official speeches and interviews, local crop and market news, child health information, and weather reports.

Basman Palace is the administrative center of the Kingdom of Jordan.

Jordanians had TV sets long before they had television produced in their own country. They could, and still can, receive programs from Damascus, Cairo, and Tel Aviv. Programming is varied, with some portion of each hour devoted to news. American, British, West German, and French films are shown, but no reruns of foreign programs. There are no commercials.

Amman has many movie theaters and there is at least one in each major town. Movies are second after radio in appeal to the population as a whole and help the illiterate portion of the population to have a greater awareness of the outside world. American and Italian films are particularly popular, as well as Arab ones produced primarily in Egypt.

Amman, with the most people, is naturally the sports center, too, although better swimming is found elsewhere. The Royal Racing Club supervises horse races at Marka in the summer and at the Dead Sea Track in the winter. The camel races are less frequent. Swimming is done at the Dead Sea, but more often at Aqaba where skin diving, water-skiing, and sailing are also possible. All Arabs are interested in physical fitness; weight lifting and physical culture clubs are popular with the young men. Boy Scout and Girl Guide troops have little opportunity for woodcraft on the barren hills and plains of Jordan, but they can drill and march and participate in encampments. Such games as tennis, Ping-Pong, track, and softball are particularly popular because they offer an opportunity for individual stardom.

One of the oldest games is *al-Minkala*. At almost every Roman campsite there is a "board" in the shape of a flat stone with two parallel rows of six shallow pits carved in it, with a larger pit at each end. Village boys do not need a board; they merely scoop out hollows in the earth and use pebbles or beans as counters. The game is played at incredible speed, bewildering to the uninitiated spectator. The idea is to move one's own counter, pit by pit, to arrive at and capture a pit full of one's opponent's counters. The key to success is one's ability at mental arithmetic, at which the Arabs excel. Trust the Nabateans, masters of finance, to complicate the game further. Occasionally in Petra one will come across a board of four parallel lines of sixteen hollows, a challenge to any mental mathematician. In the United States, the game, known as *kalah,* is available at toy stores.

Aside from the religious celebrations, there are a number of official national holidays. Arbor Day comes on January 15, when trees are planted; March 8 commemorates the coming of Feisal I to his short-lived throne in Damascus. March 22 is Arab League Day, when the charter was signed, and May 25 is Jordanian Independence Day. On August 11 King Hussein's succession to the throne is celebrated, and on November 14 his birthday. On *Shaaban* 9 of the Muslim calendar, Jordanians celebrate the Arab Revolt against Turkish rule. Other days are held important in the hearts of various groups and observance of them takes the form of noisy demonstrations. Jordanians enjoy sports events. Visiting soccer and basketball teams play exhibition games in the sports stadium in Amman with large crowds of spectators.

The government has established parks, picnic areas, and playgrounds all over the country to encourage team games and sports. Many playgrounds are built beside schools. The constitution requires children to attend school for nine years, and this takes the student through six years of primary school and three years of intermediate school. For those who can continue, three years of upper secondary school are available. The school day lasts from 8:15 to 3:30, with an hour and a half for lunch and a morning recess of fifteen minutes. Classes meet six days a week, with a half day on Thursday before the Friday Muslim Sabbath.

English is introduced in the fifth grade; otherwise subjects are similar to those in American schools except that they are taught

Two young readers discuss their Arabic textbook.

in Arabic. There are fewer special materials and textbooks, and there is a shortage of both teachers and classrooms. The classroom shortage was increased after the second wave of refugees into the Amman area after the 1967 hostilities, and many schools had to double shift. Other schools had to be reequipped, particularly on the West Bank, and the Israeli government made it difficult for teachers to return to those schools. The secondary schools divide their curriculum into two parallel courses, the literary and the scientific or technical. Exams at the end of the intermediate school determine a student's placement or whether he continues at all.

The University of Jordan opened in 1962 and has about 2,500 students. The country's largest library is on its modern campus. Other general public libraries are scattered in the major towns. Jerusalem has many special private libraries and foreign schools. There are also private schools in other parts of the country and UNRWA runs elementary and secondary schools for eighty thousand refugees on the East Bank in 153 schools, and for thirty thousand refugees on the West Bank in 86 schools. UNRWA also conducts adult classes in the camps and has a number of vocational training centers.

The Jordanian government has recognized a need to train manpower for certain industries and to relieve unemployment with taught skills. These schools are often located near where the need for workers exists, as in the case of the *al-Rubbah* Agricultural School in Kerak. Amman has several commercial schools and others are located in Irbid and Kerak. The Amman Industrial School gives courses in carpentry, plumbing, auto mechanics, electricity, and soldering. In the summer its students do field work in

Students at the University of Jordan enjoy their modern campus.

factories as semiskilled workers. The government sponsors schools for teacher training and refresher courses, and it established the Jordan Nursing College in 1955, the Midwifery and Child Care College in 1956, and the Princess Muna Nursing College in 1961.

Amman is the hub of all this national activity, education, and government. All roads lead to Amman, and all the needs of Jordanians are administered from there. It is in every sense the capital city. Amman stimulates a building boom to house all these governmental agencies and hospitals, schools, and stores for the ever-growing population. The building industry employs 17 percent of the entire work force. Some buildings are architecturally memorable, many are functional and undistinguished, and others use Islamic styles of a thousand years ago. Overlooking it all, at the citadel, is the National Museum. It displays a rich collection of archeological treasures. Well displayed and, more important, well labeled, the exhibits provide a tantalizing link between Jordan's extensive past history and the future that Amman symbolizes.

Forty miles north of Amman is Irbid. It is partly built on a *tell*, a mound of historical debris, dating to 2500 B.C., which seems to have been abandoned soon after for lack of water. Roman engineers revived the city by running conduits from a spring nearly forty miles to the east to insure a constant water supply. Some historians identify Irbid as the city of Arbila, a member of the Decapolis. It was an important stop on the caravan route from Cairo to Damascus, in any case. Today it is on the main road from Amman, forking at Irbid to go to Syria and to Iraq. Irbid is the capital of its liwa and the commercial center of a large, fertile district growing wheat, corn, fruits, and sheep.

The King's Highway south of Amman passes Madaba, most recently resettled in 1880 by Christians from Kerak. Here the famed mosaics dating from the time of the town's fifth-century Christian bishopric are still church floors. Another twenty miles south through the foothills is Dhiban, like Madaba, on a tell. Madaba has been traced back to 1300 B.C.; Dhiban to 3000 B.C. In Dhiban was found a basalt stele which unlocked Moabite history of the ninth century B.C. Next along the highway, and across the awesome canyon of Wadi Mojiba, is the town of Tafila, and beyond it Shobak. The Crusaders built the castle of Monte Reale at Shobak in A.D. 1115 to control and tax caravans moving between Damascus and Cairo. Saladin captured the castle in 1189, and what remains today is largely a fourteenth-century Mameluke restoration.

Along the fork of the road leading to Ma'an, bits of Roman paving are still visible, marked by an occasional Roman milestone. Ma'an was a railroad division point on the Hejaz Railroad where the rail line swung east and southward to Medina. For years the road south from Ma'an was a dusty track to the port of Aqaba. Now the railroad runs north from Ras al-Naqb, twenty-five miles south of Ma'an, through Amman to the Syrian border, and a good paved highway connects the end of the railroad to the port of Aqaba.

In its distant past Aqaba was important enough to have Christian bishops, one of whom entertained Caliph Omar when he visited Aqaba in A.D. 639. For a long time after that it was no more than a village with its beautiful beach, warm water for swimming and excellent fishing, unappreciated. The Arab army rested there during World War I, consolidating their position and preparing for a determined attack on the Turkish and German armies at Tafila. World War II again brought soldiers to Aqaba for rest and recreation, and the British army continued to have a camp there until 1956.

Encouraged by King Hussein, Aqaba has sports facilities for skin diving, water-skiing, and boating to capitalize on its natural features. Swimming is year-round. Aqaba is a fisherman's paradise, with such game fish as albacore, barracuda, blue tunny, kingfish, and rock cod. Since many weigh up to fifty pounds apiece, they give the sportsman a good fight. A rough-shelled crayfish, tasting like lobster, is hunted at night. On a calm day one can drift over the reefs and watch the numerous brilliantly colored small fish now being caught to adorn aquariums the world over.

After the partition of Palestine, Jordan was cut off from its long established flow of trade east to west. Shut out of the coastal ports of Haifa and Jaffa, goods had to come in through the port of Beirut. That meant that all imports bore the added expense of a long truck haul over two mountain ranges and through two countries, Lebanon and Syria, whose tariff policies were prone to fluctuate wildly. It was imperative that Jordan have its own harbor, and the sleepy village of Aqaba was jolted into activity when a jetty was built to handle deep-water ships. A firm of city planners developed a well-coordinated plan for docks, a business district, residential areas, and resort hotels. The docks can now load in an hour what it formerly took a crew one day to accomplish.

The port facilities include a deep-water wharf and four basins for loading and unloading various cargoes by lighter. Hoses unload tankers into tank farms connected to a pipeline to Jordan's oil refinery. Phosphates are loaded from an overhead elevator through a spout directly into the hold of the ship. All but the heaviest cargoes can be moved by cranes on the piers. Imports such as sugar, lumber, steel, machinery, autos and tractors, paper, cheese and milk, tea, coffee, glass, china, wool and cotton, and many consumer products are unloaded into huge warehouses, awaiting trucks to deliver them throughout the country. Aqaba is a busy port and an efficient one, able to handle any size ship in some way or other.

The recreational attractions of the East Bank of Jordan are balanced by the places of religious pilgrimage on the West Bank.

The "little town of Bethlehem" sprawls atop two hills that provide it a triangular base. On the north and south the hillsides are steep, and the gardens and orchards have to be terraced. To the east, the fields slope gently toward the Dead Sea. Central to the town is the Latin Church of the Nativity, as sacred to Christians as the Holy Sepulchre in Jerusalem. The basilica was started by Queen Helena in 326 and finished seven years later, built over the grotto that had been the long-cherished site of the manger. Two centuries later it was rebuilt by Justinian with mosaic floors that survive in the present church.

When the Persians invaded Palestine in A.D. 614 and destroyed Jersalem, they spared the Church of the Nativity. According to legend a mosaic showing the Three Wise Men in Persian costume staved off destruction. By the time the Crusaders arrived, the church was badly in need of repair. They decorated the interior and on Christmas Day, 1100, crowned Baldwin king of the new Latin Kingdom of Jerusalem.

Through the centuries various Christian sects have fought, not always without bloodshed, for the custody of the church. Finally, in the nineteenth century, the sultan of Constantinople issued a decree establishing a *status quo* for all faiths in Palestine. It was high time someone took control. In 1847 the silver star marking the spot of the manger disappeared and was never found. The resulting quarrel over which group should replace it provoked intervention by Napoleon III and Sultan Abdul Mejid, who had the present star sealed in place in 1853.

On December twenty-fourth it is the custom for various groups to walk from Jerusalem to Bethlehem, going by different routes. Led by churchmen and patriarchs, the robed priests, the choirboys, the bands, and the thousands of pilgrims make the procession a memorable pageant. Each procession acquires new pilgrims along the way and, meeting at Rachel's tomb outside Bethlehem, they proceed together to the Church of the Nativity. The same brilliant pageant is repeated thirteen days later by the Greek Orthodox and Eastern churches. Again the variety of rich vestments, the uniforms of the different orders, the banners, the choirs and bands attract spectators from all faiths. On January 19 the Armenians have their festive turn. The Protestants do not maintain a chapel in the Church of the Nativity, so on Christmas Eve they borrow the little Greek church of St. George and hold a Church of England service at midnight. There are also services at dusk in Shepherd's Field below the town and carol-singing in the Church of the Nativity courtyard between services. For those few nights of Christmas, Bethlehem rings with joy and the song of the angels.

Hebron commands the sector south of Jerusalem, on steep hills of 3,500 feet elevation. In early times Hebron was the southernmost stronghold of the Hittites and was called *Membre*. When Abraham was moving his family and flocks westward, he stayed for ten years in the environs before moving on to Beersheba. While at Membre, he entered into elaborate negotiations to buy a burial ground for his people. After protracted bargaining, Abraham secured the field and cave of *Machpelah*.

Within the modern city is a mosque built on the traditional site of the cave. The lower part was built by Herod, the main walls of today were a Crusader basilica on top of a Byzantine church, and the upper part with its minarets was added by the Mamelukes. Arabs call it "Sacred to Abraham, the Friend of God." On either side of the entrance are cenotaphs, or empty tombs, honoring Sarah and Abraham. In front of the mihrab, or prayer niche, are the cenotaphs of Isaac and Rebecca, and of Jacob and Leah. The cenotaphs are draped with heavy green velvet covers embroidered with gold threads. Beneath, in the cave under the floor, the patriarchs are buried.

Because of its association with Abraham, the Muslims made Hebron a fourth sacred city, and many pilgrims have visited it ever since. In more recent times it has been one of the Jordanian liwa centers. A large concentration of Palestinian refugees settled around Hebron after the 1948 war, but many of them have now moved to the East Bank.

There are many small industries in Hebron. One is soap, made of the oil from the olive groves in the Nablus region and the potash from the Dead Sea which Hebron overlooks. Another is leather, which has been a Hebron industry for centuries. In 1961 the Jordan Tanning Company built a factory with modern machinery to update this traditional craft. Glassblowing is another Hebron skill practiced for many generations. Graceful shapes in bright green, deep blue-green, amber, and soft purple glass find their way into many homes.

Over the years the peasants and craftsmen preserved traditional songs, continued to weave and pot by custom and usage. Villages had their poets and musicians to improvise songs for local celebrations and holidays. These folk arts are still practiced today, often encouraged by music and dance festivals or by the international interest in arts and crafts. In 1962 the then mayor of Jerusalem, Raouli al-Khatib, and his wife encouraged the opening of a permanent exhibition and salesroom for Jordanian crafts. This center was well supported by craftsmen and customers alike.

Village embroidery of Palestine is rich in designs, and so is the inlay work in wood, bone, and mother-of-pearl that seems to carry on the tradition of mosaics. Mother-of-pearl carving is unique to Bethlehem, a long way from a shell-filled beach. The glazed tile and ceramic studios of Jerusalem developed as suppliers for repairs to the Dome of the Rock, and in 1966 supplied glazed tile street signs for the Old City. Basalt from the Dead Sea, turned on a wheel like pottery, forms bowls and vases in classic shapes. The same is done with olive wood, although it is also carved. Black coral from the waters of the Gulf of Aqaba makes beads for prayer strings. Usually found in the Red Sea, King Hussein discovered it at Aqaba one day while he was skin diving. Another craft responsive to the pilgrims is the candlemaking of Jerusalem. The wide, flat, paddle-shaped candles have many wicks and are covered with gold tracery. Tradition calls this candle "the palm," and a bride held one in each hand while she danced before her bridegroom.

North of Jerusalem, in the mountains of old Samaria, lies Nablus, another population center. It is between two mountains on the pass from east to west, thirty-two miles north of Jerusalem. The city is an attractive cluster of stone houses set in groves of trees with many springs cascading from pool to pool down the mountainsides. Groves of walnuts, almonds, pears, plums, and pomegranates provide a variety of foods as well as shade. The olive groves are the most extensive, the source for a modern olive oil refinery.

Nablus is relatively new as a city, built by the Emperor Vespasian after he had crushed the Jewish rebellion in A.D. 70. He called it Neapolis, new town, to distinguish it from ancient Schechem a mile away. An American expedition in 1957 uncovered a great many things of historical interest. Schechem was an important city as early as 3500 B.C., and many invaders recognized its strategic importance. Fortresses and palaces guarded the pass between Mt. Girizim and Mt. Ebal. The Hyksos, who brought with them the horse and the war chariot, dominated Jordan and Egypt until about 1500 B.C. Then the fortress city seems to have slowly lost its importance and was ignored in the building of the new city of Nablus.

One little village near Nablus shelters about three hundred members of the Samaritan sect. They are a dwindling remnant of Arab tribesmen captured by the Assyrians in 715 B.C. They were sent to Samaria where they mixed with the earlier colonists from Assyria. Adopting the Jewish religion, they had also absorbed some religious ideas from their Assyrian neighbors. When the Jews returned from their "Babylonian captivity," they refused to recognize the Samaritans as truly Jewish and left them to wither on their own sectarian vine.

The people of Jericho live in the shadow of the Mount of Temptation. On this mountain Jesus prayed for forty days and forty nights, tempted to lead an earthly kingdom but refusing. The spring which feeds the oasis, Elisha's Fountain, is at the foot of the mountain. Within the area fed by its water is a lush tropical "island" of palm trees, yellow acacia, and orange flame trees. It is the fruit garden of Jordan, and winter vegetables grown under irrigation have a six weeks' market advantage. Figs, oranges, and bananas flourish as they must have for the tables of Herod the Great at his nearby winter palace or for Zaccheus when Jesus shared a meal with him. The largest community of Palestinian refugees settled around Jericho before 1967, but now that UNRWA camp is a ghost town and the refugees have moved to Amman.

11

Weaving the Future

A skillful and creative handweaver uses all the odd bits of yarn at hand. Some have been left over from another project, others are of an unusual color or texture, but the yarns are only successful in the new design because of the overall pattern. Traditional Palestinian weaving often meant several weavers working on the same large piece, on looms pegged flat above the ground. Yarns were left to dry after dyeing by spreading them on a rocky beach. The weavers improvised with what they had.

The threads in Jordanian life offer just such a creative challenge, if they are to be woven into a durable, well-designed whole. The conflicting aims of Jordan nationalists and Palestinians and the great need for economic development in a country with few natural resources are facts, but so is the largely Muslim population in a basically agricultural country. With planning, many believe that the present population can be supported on the small wedge of fertile land. Jordan is committed to make her plans come true.

In 1948 the Arab League reported about the Palestinians: "They have not been able to plan for the future, because the very fact of their having a future in Palestine has been in doubt." In the case of the Jordanians, much the same could be said. The government has made the plans but conditions have made them invalid. Jordan's Seven Year Program for the period April 1, 1964, to March 31, 1971, listed basic assumptions for its success, one of which was "political stability, both internal and external . . . for the entire period." In 1948 Jordan's population was increased threefold without a corresponding increase in resources. The unusual pressures Jordan faced forced a complete rerouting of trade and communication lines. Traditional ports on the Mediterranean had to be replaced by developing Aqaba. Roads had to be built north and south to handle the shift in traffic patterns. Airports were built for the new air age. In 1967 Jordan lost control of the West Bank, including almost a third of its arable land and nearly half the population. It also lost its principal foreign-currency producing industry, tourism.

The Arab countries showed their displeasure with Jordan with an economic boycott after the final crackdown on the Palestinian commandos in July, 1971. Libya and Kuwait cut off their annual subsidies; only Saudi Arabia didn't break its pledge to Jordan. Iraq and Syria closed their borders with Jordan and prohibited Jordanian airliners from overflying Syrian and Iraqi airspace. This affected the movement of both trade and people. The deficit was greater than anticipated and internal revenues were lower in 1971 because of lower development allocations, too. A year of drought caused poor crops and a 25 percent decrease in agricultural profit. In order to counter the trend, Jordan cut off expenditures to the West Bank, including paying the salaries of Jordanian civil servants now working for the Israelis. A law for 1972 requires Jordanian expatriates, mainly in Kuwait and the Gulf states, to pay an annual income tax of 7 percent.

With greater political stability, which is King Hussein's priority, work on development projects can resume. Already the Trans-Arabian pipeline (TAPline) has increased its transit royalties on the pipeline crossing Jordan on its way from Dhahran, Saudi Arabia, to Sidon, Lebanon. Work can move ahead on a satellite communications ground station being built by a Japanese firm. Jordan can tackle the development of its fishing industry with a grant from the United Nations Special Fund.

Jordan planners recognize the need for outside help, both from grants and investments and from foreign specialists. Jordan has a high percentage of students specializing in foreign universities. They are needed to develop Jordan and to bring new techniques to apply to old problems. Jordan is a member of the International Monetary Fund and the World Bank, and gets aid from Arab League members as well as from the United States, Britain, and West Germany. Now or never, these resources are needed for peaceful uses. The Central Bank of Jordan and the Ministry of Finance have wide authority to manage money matters in the country and among the commercial banks. There is also a large system of approximately seven hundred farm cooperatives for marketing, technical advice, and banking; there are government loan services for improving crops and seed stocks. The monetary unit is the *dinar,* made up of one thousand *fils,* par with the pound sterling. It still circulates on the West Bank as well as in unoccupied Jordan.

King Hussein gambled in 1956 when he asked the British to leave and discontinue their special relationship with Jordan and its army. Britain cut its aid and, much to everyone's surprise, Jordan was able to manage economically without it. Today the resources are fewer but the same sort of appraisal of possibilities and alternatives is being made by the government. Phosphate mining is being increased. Marble cutting and finishing is being developed as an industrial craft to complement Jordan's exports in limestone and cement. Fertilizer is Jordan's biggest export but the rich deposits of potash in the Dead Sea await wider world marketing.

The East Bank, before 1967, did not consume as many imported items as the West Bank, and the savings on these imports is said to balance the loss in tourist income. Jordan has so far been geared to the pilgrim tourist, with other sights visited as an afterthought to the shrines of Jerusalem. The East Bank alone has many unique sights to offer the tourist, spectacular on their own merit. Petra has no rival, and there are few Roman cities better preserved than Jerash. The hunting lodges and palaces of the caliphs are seldom visited by Jordanians or foreigners, and are wonderful haunted houses for the desert camper to investigate.

The first national park in Jordan, al-Azrak Desert Park, is fifty

The oasis of Azrak is Jordan's first national park.

miles east of Amman. It is an oasis with many groves of palm trees. Swampy water gives temporary homes to ducks, geese, teal, and snipe on their migratory flights. Many stone hand-axes of two hundred thousand years ago have been found in ancient irrigation channels, but most of this history is hidden. Of more modern interest is a handsome black basalt castle with Greek and Latin inscriptions. Later it was a Muslim fort during the Crusader period. According to an inscription over a door, Aybak was governor there from 1213 to 1238, a long rule for those days.

Kerak used to be known as the castle with its own port on the Dead Sea. Perhaps it can be known as such again, offering a swimming alternative on the route to Aqaba. The port of Aqaba offers both unlimited water sports and the opportunity for scientific observations. The pilgrimages devout Muslims made a thousand years ago often turned into scientific expeditions. Observations were made, records were kept, and information was exchanged with other pilgrims. The obvious area of learning was geography but this often led into astronomy or botany. Care was taken to obtain accurate information, and special scholars were often sought out along the way. Even to this day the names of these scientists are not well known to us but what they learned and spread is the basis of much modern knowledge. The University of Jordan has a great tradition on which to build and a laboratory of geological and historical specimens at its doorstep.

There is a never-ending need for experiments with drought-resisting plants and terracing and subsoiling measures to retain moisture. Without the West Bank, Jordan lost a major source of farm produce. The extended shelling in the East Ghor region, the other agricultural section, held up the planting of crops, caused crop loss, damaged the irrigation system, and hindered work on the extension of the canal. The winter crop is barley or wheat; the summer crop is melons or tomatoes. Vegetables and

fruit are raised in irrigated areas, and wheat can be raised in mar-
ginal land, some of which could profitably be returned to pasture.
A new dry-land strain of wheat has improved the yield as have
better fertilizers, pest control, and seed selection.

The main crops are wheat, barley, lentils, beans, sorghum, ses-
ame, tobacco, and maize; olives, grapes, figs and, with irrigation,
bananas, citrus fruits, and dates. Other foods are imported, including sugar, cheese, milk, tea and coffee, eggs and wheat.

Since 1950 the Arab Development Society has been experi-
menting with farmland near Jericho, first finding freshwater wells
where none was known to exist, then cleansing the soil of the salt
density caused by nearness to the Dead Sea, and finally working
out methods to give maximum yield in their particular growing
conditions. Alfalfa turned out to be the best crop, and sprinklers
the best means of irrigation. This farm experimented also with
poultry raising and was among the first to grade eggs. Dairy herds
were carefully bred, and the milk was widely distributed. Musa
Alami, the director, has never stopped expanding the possibilities
of the farm. It was the pioneer in ice cream production for Jordan, and its fresh vegetables were flown to Beirut and other
places weekly.

At the same time, Musa Alami made a home for orphan refugee
boys, setting up a school and vocational training center. Refugee
farmers in nearby Jericho were hired to run the farm and, as time
went on, more and more acres were washed free of salt and put
under cultivation. What to plant? That, too, was an unending experiment for better methods and better crops. Disturbances
which rocked Jordan in 1956 found a target in the Jericho area at
the Arab Development Society farm and school. The school
buildings and dormitories, the barns and workshops, were burned
and looted. Musa Alami was not to be defeated; he rebuilt, with
the help of a growing number of admirers around the world. The

Former lawyer Musa Alami watches some of his boys swim in the irrigation reservoir at the experimental farm and school at Jericho.

boys were coming to live and learn at the farm for six-year periods, and then either going on to college or out into the valley or beyond with the training to assure them of jobs. They also had the love and interest of their "uncle" Musa, which had given them that special confidence which only a real home can achieve. In the political and social uncertainties of the Palestinian population in the Jericho valley, Musa Alami has been a unique influence and a tower of strength in times of adversity.

The farm was in the line of fire during and after the 1967 conflict with Israel and is now in occupied territory. Every night there was an alert and the older boys carried the younger boys into the emergency bomb shelters. Finally the younger boys were transferred, with their teachers and books, to a new school nearer Jerusalem, built for Palestinian refugees by Kuwaitis. The vocational-training courses continue at the farm for the older boys, and fields irrigated with sprinklers continue to produce alfalfa and other crops. It is not easy to live in such a strategic spot and pretend that life is the same. Import restrictions by the Israeli government make it difficult to get farm machinery; Jerusalem is sealed off by the Israelis, and Amman by the demarcation line. The once-pretty campus lost its fast-growing eucalyptus trees in the 1967 war, and many of the stone buildings with their palm-frond awnings were damaged beyond usefulness.

Many other Palestinians have taught vocation classes, operated craft studios, or instructed mothers in nutrition and baby care for their less fortunate refugee neighbors, helping them to help themselves. Out of its small national budget, Jordan took official responsibility for those refugee farmers who possessed their houses but whose fields were in Israeli-held territory. Technically not refugees, since they still had homes, they could not receive help from UNRWA nor could they farm land to support themselves.

Some of these refugee farmers are now enthusiastically employed on the repairs to the East Ghor Canal. Ghor is the Arab word for the Jordan valley, and the canal is an irrigation system for the sixty-five-mile-long Ghor. Dams on the Yarmuk and at Zarqa catch and hold winter floods. The water is diverted through a tunnel 460 feet long into a forty-three-mile-long concrete-lined canal, built by American machinery and watering a strip three to five miles wide. From the main canal, smaller canals spread out into an eventual one hundred thousand acres. The Ghor system uses pumps and animal power as well as gravity flow. There are more tributaries into the Jordan from the east than the west, and it may be possible to dam other wadis as time goes on.

Joint ventures by the government and private capital have built textile mills, a cement plant, and factories manufacturing paints, cosmetics, wet batteries, and vegetable oils. Detergents,

A tunnel was cut to divert the water of the Yarmuk River into the East Ghor Canal.

soaps, matches, cigarettes, and shoe leather are all produced in Jordan. The Arab Potash Company is located at Safi; the oil refinery at Zarqa where crude oil is piped in by TAPline. In 1966 a pharmaceutical plant was built at Salt to repackage imported drugs. Amman has a thriving industry in clay pipe, roof tiles, and firebricks from the local clay. Textiles, domestically woven at the Jordan worsted mills from imported cotton and wool, hold distinct promise for expansion. Other industries are food canning, dairy products, ceramics, and the preparation of fertilizers. Foreign investors are encouraged, Jordanian industries are protected from competition, imports for equipment are eased, and technical advice is sought. Jordan offers a good climate for industrial growth.

Jordan also offers a potentially good climate for cultural expression. There has been little time, with the long-lasting and diverse political struggles, for creative thinking in the years of Hussein's reign. It has been very difficult for musical composers, poets, novelists, and painters to "do their thing." Poetry of revolution and suppression among the Palestinians has been the most widespread expression of the contemporary scene. Painters of the Mandate period, trained in France or Russia, are recognized be-

The phosphate industry processes Jordan's major natural resources.

yond Jordan's boundaries but they do not represent Jordan today. Kamal Boulatta, a Palestinian, has international stature as a painter, using Islamic calligraphy as one of his sources of expression. There is much more in Jordan's cultural heritage for Jordanian artists to tap.

Because of the political turmoil, the poster has become the primary art form. Posters by Jordanian and Palestinian artists can be seen throughout the Arab world. They are well-designed and have a message with a punch. An Arab-wide fiction contest, sponsored by a Lebanese magazine, was won in 1968 by two Jordanians, Ameen Shunnar and Tayseer Sboul. Others have won recognition in another country first, partly because there are more opportunities for publication outside of Jordan than within.

Many writers have had their best creative opportunity in Jordan by preparing scripts for Jordan radio or television, particularly for holidays or about current social problems. There have also been many translations of plays from other languages and countries, because the Islamic tradition is for mimicry and storytelling rather than formal theater. Radio has also offered opportunities for musical composers.

Each radio station has a *takht,* or small instrumental ensemble, to accompany singers or interpret musical classics. It is composed of an *oud,* a version of the lute; a *qanum,* rather like a zither with sixty-four strings over a flat trapezoidal box; a *nay,* which is a single-reeded cane flute; a *daff,* or tambourine; a *durbakkeh,* which is a vase-shaped earthenware drum with a skin drumhead played with the fingers; plus a violin and a Western flute.

Two other common Arab musical instruments are ancestors of Western instruments: the *rababa* is a one- or two-string viol, and the *naggara,* or kettledrums, were originally a small pair of copper ceremonial drums. Arab music uses quarter tones and complex rhythmical patterns that produce a mournful, haunting undertone to the music. It may be sorrowful or spirited, dance music or marching music, but its range is subtle for Western ears.

Music, painting, and literature have all been restricted by the military upheavals, the political tensions, the economic hardships, and the traditionalism of many Jordanians. As more Jordanians are better educated this will change, but complete artistic expression will probably not occur until women are educated as generally as men. At present, despite the laws for compulsory education, half as many girls as boys receive primary education. Women do not vote, either. Despite these limitations, many women are active in public life, particularly in the field of social welfare, and there are many national women's organizations affiliated with their international counterparts.

The first national fine arts festival was planned for 1967 in Jerash but it was cancelled by the war. Jordan shared the Dead Sea Scrolls twice on world tour; in 1964 at the New York World's Fair, and touring museums in Britain and the United States in 1966. The international trend now is for national treasures to stay at home and lure visitors to see them. The wear and tear on the world's cultural treasures has been too great to continue the practice of lending them on tour. In Jordan's case there is much more to see that can't be moved and enlarges man's understanding of himself.

The long history of the Arabs as cultured, intelligent people, with achievements in every branch of science, law, and the arts, is a special heritage. This heritage of the past strengthens and endows the people of Jordan to meet the challenges of today with confidence and success. Particularly it challenges the young people. Their whole lives have been spent in a climate of uncertainties and failures. They know that Arab unity is a fragile thing because many countries think kings are old-fashioned, and they work as much against Jordan as with it. The fedayeen had their chance to right wrongs by force and got valuable publicity for the cause. This has cleared the way for a more moderate approach by more moderate Palestinians to make their voices heard in a peace settlement. Before a new faction tries to speak for the whole, Jordan has the opportunity to build a strong country. It has met the most extreme tests of a nation and survived.

Without the 1967 war, Jordan would have been self-sufficient by 1972. Its goal of agricultural independence would have been realized. Now the fertile farms on the West Bank are out of reach and largely untilled. There is little more land to be cultivated on the East Bank, even with the optimum reach of the East Ghor system. Jordan's other immediate goal is developing foreign investment which is limited by shipping restrictions and sparse natural resources. With the Suez Canal closed, shipments to and from Aqaba are much more costly to Europe and North America. With Syrian restrictions on use of airspace and land transit, Jordan is hemmed in on the north. On the west, Israel is an uncompromising neighbor, and Israel flourishes at Jordan's expense.

It is ironic and tragic that in attempting to right a wrong to one group, the Jews, the world caused injustice to another, the Arabs. The Palestinians became victims of war and terror and homeless helplessness to make way for the Zionists. The Palestinians are paying a penalty for something neither of their making nor their responsibility. They have lived in makeshift camps, not for a night or a month, for almost twenty-five years. It is a life of squalor, stench, quarrels, and rags.

Jordan, unlike other Arab countries, granted full citizenship to the Palestinians. It included them in the government and gave them jobs on an equal footing with other Jordanians. Their skills were utilized when it was possible. But seldom in world history has there been such a tremendous economic problem for a new nation to face as that of trying to assimilate the one-third of its population that were homeless, destitute, and unemployable. Just before the June, 1967, conflict there were still 720,000 refugees registered with UNRWA. Of these, 233,000 were in camps on the West Bank and 400,000 were receiving food, but lived in their own homes without a source of self-support. This was a third of Jordan's total 2,100,000 citizens. In February, 1968, the refugees on the East Bank had swelled to 593,000, of whom 240,000 had crossed the Jordan River after the June, 1967, war. This still leaves about one-third of Jordan's population on the West Bank, or 690,000 people. All of the refugees are suffering greater hardships than before, because the services and housing of the West Bank were left behind and are of no use either to the refugees or to UNRWA. The Jordanians who still live on the West Bank also suffer greater hardships, because the Israelis are not recognizing the international laws which govern a situation of occupation.

The limits of Jordan's bargaining power and the ultimate limits of its resources are evident. There are certain things the rest of the world must do. Its alternatives are either to subsidize Jordan forever or to force a fair settlement that gives Jordan the means to be independent and self-sufficient.

The majority of Jordanians have accepted the November 22, 1967, United Nations Resolution on a settlement with Israel. The members of the United Nations Security Council unanimously supported the Resolution, but so far it has been words, words, words, and only a grudging dole in the form of UNRWA to keep alive the Palestinian refugees at a subsistence level. The world, as the United Nations, rushed to right the wrongs done to the Jews by setting up Israel as a country. Now it must take firm action to see that no further abuses happen and to heed the Palestinian cry for justice.

The United Nations Resolution commits the member nations to (1) withdrawal of Israeli armed forces from the occupied territories, (2) freedom of navigation through international waterways, and (3) a just settlement of the refugee problem. This means resettlement of the refugees or compensation for their losses; the United Nations record is very clear on this point. Jerusalem is also part of the negotiation; for Israel to say that "Jerusalem is not negotiable" is to defy the entire basis of partition to make room for the Jews in Palestine. This Resolution disallows one country from swallowing up another, because each must recognize the "sovereignty, territorial integrity, and political independence" of the others. The Resolution summarizes all that has gone before in negotiating the problems of the Middle East and in trying to unscramble the mess the United Nations created by establishing Israel. The rest of the world needs to make good its endorsement of these principles and give diplomatic rather than military assistance to Jordan and her neighbors.

In today's world no nation stands alone, no matter how powerful, and no nation can afford to ignore the rights of others. In various ways, this is what the people of the world are saying as they strive for independence from colonial powers or secede as minorities from new national structures. The violence that has too often been the tool for achieving such change is an indication of an unheeding world. Cooperative action has been defeated in many places in the last decade, simply because an easy solution has been adopted which neither solved the problem nor understood the dispute. Jordan asks the world to listen carefully and to act supportively. The strands to weave into a peaceful tomorrow for Jordan depend on peace itself. Peace is the warp thread of Jordan's fabric.

Index

About the Authors

Paul Copeland moved with his family from New York City to Washington State when he was twelve. He was graduated from Whitman College and spent two years teaching English at the American University of Beirut in Lebanon. He returned to teaching after practicing architecture for several years, and after receiving his master's degree in history from the University of Washington. He taught history in the Seattle public schools for many years and at Aleppo College in Syria for four years in the 1950's. He is also the author of *The Land and People of Syria* and *The Land and People of Libya*.

Frances Copeland Stickles, the daughter of Paul Copeland, is a former school and children's librarian. In 1958, after her return from teaching in Lebanon, she published a book for children called *Land Between*. She is now president of Middle East Exhibits and Training in Washington, D.C. She is married to a lawyer and they have a daughter and a son.